HOUSE COMMITTEE ON SMALL BUSINESS

SAM GRAVES, Missouri, *Chairman*
STEVE CHABOT, Ohio
STEVE KING, Iowa
MIKE COFFMAN, Colorado
BLAINE LUETKEMEYER, Missouri
MICK MULVANEY, South Carolina
SCOTT TIPTON, Colorado
JAIME HERRERA BEUTLER, Washington
RICHARD HANNA, New York
TIM HUELSKAMP, Kansas
DAVID SCHWEIKERT, Arizona
KERRY BENTIVOLIO, Michigan
CHRIS COLLINS, New York
TOM RICE, South Carolina
NYDIA VELÁZQUEZ, New York, *Ranking Member*
KURT SCHRADER, Oregon
YVETTE CLARKE, New York
JUDY CHU, California
JANICE HAHN, California
DONALD PAYNE, JR., New Jersey
GRACE MENG, New York
BRAD SCHNEIDER, Illinois
RON BARBER, Arizona
ANN McLANE KUSTER, New Hampshire
PATRICK MURPHY, Florida

LORI SALLEY, *Staff Director*
PAUL SASS, *Deputy Staff Director*
BARRY PINELES, *Chief Counsel*
MICHAEL DAY, *Minority Staff Director*

CONTENTS

OPENING STATEMENTS

WITNESSES

APPENDIX

BITCOIN: EXAMINING THE BENEFITS AND RISKS FOR SMALL BUSINESS

WEDNESDAY, APRIL 2, 2014

HOUSE OF REPRESENTATIVES,
COMMITTEE ON SMALL BUSINESS,
Washington, DC.

The Committee met, pursuant to call, at 1:00 p.m., in Room 2360, Rayburn House Office Building. Hon. Sam Graves [chairman of the Committee] presiding.

Present: Representatives Graves, Chabot, Luetkemeyer, Mulvaney, Tipton, Hanna, Huelskamp, Schweikert, Velázquez, Clarke, Payne, Meng, and Mclane Kuster.

Mr. TIPTON. [Presiding] Good afternoon. This hearing will come to order. Chairman Graves will be joining us shortly. I will fill in for him here in the interim.

I would like to thank all of our witnesses for taking the time to be able to join us here today.

To be able to gain an advantage in an increasingly competitive marketplace, small businesses are looking for innovative ways to be able to cut costs and be able to gain access to customers. One small way the businesses are doing this is through the use of cutting-edge technologies that can provide efficiencies, and Bitcoins may be one of these innovative technologies.

Bitcoins are a form of virtual currency first introduced in 2008 that allows users to exchange value digitally through the Internet. Despite not being backed by a government or holding any intrinsic value of their own, Bitcoins are growing as an alternative payment method. This hearing will examine the benefits and risks associated with Bitcoin as a payment system for all small businesses.

While the origins of Bitcoin remain mysterious, it has grown rapidly in the last few years. Businesses choose to accept Bitcoin for many reasons, including to be at the forefront of new technology, to attract customers now using Bitcoin, to lower transaction fees from credit and debit cards, and to eliminate certain kinds of fraud.

Despite these advantages, there are numerous risks that small businesses should consider before implementing a Bitcoin payment system. These risks include volatility of price, security and policy uncertainty. Further, recent developments in the Bitcoin industry have cast a shadow on its security and sustainability. Hacking attacks have led to the downfall of a leading Bitcoin exchange company, while its use for criminal activity has led to greater scrutiny by law enforcement and other federal and state banking regulators.

We have invited a distinguished panel of experts who will explain what Bitcoin is, and we appreciate that, and how it operates, why it might be a good fit for small businesses and what the risks are associated with Bitcoin. We hope that by providing information about Bitcoin, small businesses will be in a better position to know whether adopting Bitcoin as a payment system might be a way for small businesses to be able to gain more customers. This hearing will also inform Members as we consider implications of policies affecting the use of virtual currencies.

With that, I would again like to thank our distinguished panel of witnesses for joining us here today, and I now recognize the ranking member for her opening statement.

Ms. VELAZQUEZ. Thank you, Mr. Chairman. Good afternoon, everyone, and thank you for being here today.

American entrepreneurship is closely linked to technology called innovation. Whether it was the arrival of Google or Facebook, the widespread use of smartphone apps or cloud computing, our nation's entrepreneurs drive many technological developments. Not only do small firms help create new technologies that drive growth, but they often benefit from new systems and processes.

The relatively recent arrival of digital currencies is one technology that presents significant opportunity. Just as the Internet has empowered entrepreneurs to reach new global markets and identify more efficient ways of doing business, digital currencies like Bitcoin can save small firms on transaction costs. For a small company accepting major credit cards, each card swipe can cost as much as one-quarter of a cent in addition to having to return 3 to 6 percent of sales total to the credit card company. Some credit card companies also charge businesses to join the network. By contrast, when utilizing Bitcoin, there is no cost of joining the network. Fees are less than 1 percent. For large retailers and big box stores, this cost may sound minor, but among small companies operating on thin margins, those expenditures are up. Moreover, should currencies like Bitcoin become widely utilized, they could create competitive pressure for conventional financial institutions to lower transaction fees in an effort to retain small business customers.

Beyond allowing small firms to save on transaction costs, Bitcoins offer consumers other advantages. For customer seeking anonymity, Bitcoins provide more privacy than credit card transactions. Small firms are gradually recognizing the promise of accepting Bitcoins. In 2012, about 1,000 businesses used BitPay, the largest processor of Bitcoin payments. Today, more than 13,000 small businesses in the U.S. employ this service. While most are online sellers, one in five are traditional brick-and-mortar operations suggesting the technology is gaining broader acceptance.

Although this growth sounds promising, a number of unanswered questions might be impeding small businesses' use of Bitcoins. Price fluctuation for Bitcoins create complications. Last spring, Bitcoin's dollar exchange rate rose sharply from $50 to $350 and then fell to $70. With swings like this, one has to wonder whether small businesses will find it difficult to continually price and reprice their products in order to ensure they receive fair compensation from customers.

There are also security questions. Hacking incidents in 2012 and 2013 endangered many users' Bitcoins. More recently, the bankruptcy of Mt. Gox, one of the largest Bitcoin exchanges, was followed by news that the company has lost hundreds of millions of dollars in Bitcoins. For small businesses to fully benefit from this currency, customers must be assured their money is safe and cannot be snatched out of cyberspace. It also remains to be seen how the IRS's recent ruling declaring Bitcoin a property as opposed to a currency will impact this technology growth.

In all these areas, the Committee has an obligation to ensure small business interests are taking into account. We want small firms to benefit from this technology, but we must see to it that there are safeguards protecting them and their customers. Likewise, we must see that tax regulatory changes do not preclude the use of this currency.

I expect today's hearing will help us learn about complex issues like this and assist the Committee as it addresses such matters going forward. In that regard, I would like to thank our witnesses for being here, and I yield the balance of my time.

Mr. TIPTON. Thank you, Ms. Velázquez.

If Committee members have an opening statement prepared, I ask that they submit it for the record.

I would like to take a moment just to be able to explain our timing lights. You will each have five minutes for your testimony. The light will start out as green. When you get into the danger zone is when it moves to yellow. When it gets to the red, if you would conclude your statements at that time we would appreciate it.

So again, thank you, gentlemen, for joining us this afternoon.

Our first witness is Mr. Jerry Brito, senior research fellow at Mercatus Center at George Mason University. Mr. Brito focuses his research on technology, Internet policy, copyright, and regulatory process. Mr. Brito is the coauthor of Bitcoin: A Primer for Policymakers.

Mr. Brito, thank you for being here, and I look forward to your testimony.

STATEMENTS OF JERRY BRITO, SENIOR RESEARCH FELLOW, MERCATUS CENTER, GEORGE MASON UNIVERSITY; ADAM WHITE, DIRECTOR OF BUSINESS DEVELOPMENT AND SALES, COINBASE; MARK WILLIAMS, EXECUTIVE-IN-RESIDENCE, MASTER LECTURER, BOSTON UNIVERSITY, SCHOOL OF MANAGEMENT; L. MICHAEL COUVILLION, ASSOCIATE PROFESSOR OF ECONOMICS, PLYMOUTH STATE UNIVERSITY, COLLEGE OF BUSINESS ADMINISTRATION

STATEMENT OF JERRY BRITO

Mr. BRITO. Thank you. Thank you very much, Mr. Chairman, members of the Committee. Thank you for inviting me here today to comment on Bitcoin's use for small businesses.

Virtual currencies and electronic payment systems are nothing new. They have existed for decades. So what is it about Bitcoin that makes it unique? Bitcoin is the world's first completely decentralized digital currency, and it is the decentralized part that makes it unique. Prior to Bitcoin's invention in 2009, online currencies or payment systems had to be managed by a central authority, whether it was Facebook issuing Facebook credits or

PayPal ensuring that transactions between its customers were reconciled. However, by ingeniously solving some longstanding problems in computer science, Bitcoin for the first time makes possible electronic transactions that are person-to-person without the need for an intermediary between them, just like cash.

This technical breakthrough presents both potential benefits and risks for consumers and small businesses. For example, because there is no central intermediary in Bitcoin transactions, fees associated with those transactions are relatively small. Small businesses accepting credit card payments often face fees of around 25 cents for each card swipe plus 2 to 4 percent of the transaction total. If you are a small margin business, those fees can really eat into your bottom-line. In contrast, businesses that use a merchant processor, like BitPay or Coinbase, pay fees of 1 percent or less on Bitcoin transactions. If you are a smaller margin business, that difference could mean doubling your profits.

Another reason small businesses are attracted to Bitcoin is that, like cash, all transactions are final. And again, because there is no central intermediary, there is no third party that can reverse the transaction. This protects small businesses from chargeback fraud, which often results not just in the loss of a sale but also in penalty fees. And such friendly fraud accounts for 41 percent of all claims. And if a merchant has 1 percent of their charges reversed as chargebacks, they can often be kicked out of the credit card networks, potentially ending their business.

And finally, because Bitcoin is decentralized, businesses can now accept international payments that were not previously possible. There are over 50 countries that traditional payment processors do not serve, often because of high fraud rates. Because Bitcoin payments are global and final, doing business with consumers in those countries, especially in developing countries is now feasible.

For consumers, the benefit Bitcoin presents is essentially choice. Wishing to encourage its use, merchants frequently offer discounts to customers who pay with Bitcoin. This means consumers will be able to choose to pay a little more and get the benefits of using a credit card, like fraud insurance and airline miles, or they can choose to pay a little less by using Bitcoin. For some price-sensitive consumers, this could be a very valuable choice.

Of course, there are also risks associated with Bitcoin. Chief among these is Bitcoin's historic volatility. It has traded from a low of pennies when it was first introduced in 2009, to a high of $1,200 last December, with wild short-term swings. However, there is nothing inherent in Bitcoin's design that naturally makes it so extremely volatile. Its extreme volatility is likely attributable to the fact that it is a new currency. Bitcoin is still an experiment, and it is still in the process of discovering a more stable price.

Additionally, as a nascent currency, it is very thinly traded, and as a result, a single, large enough trade can affect the exchange price substantially. If Bitcoin's use continues to expand, potentially, we could expect to see extreme volatility subside. Additionally, derivatives that allow investors to bet against the price of Bitcoin will soon become available and this should help stabilize the price as well.

The volatility risk is one that a small business faces if it accepts Bitcoins directly. It should be noted, however, that small businesses can use Bitcoin entirely as a payment system without ever holding Bitcoins. And in fact, this is what most small businesses do. Using a merchant service company like BitPay or Coinbase, merchants can denominate prices in dollars, not in Bitcoin, and denominate their prices in dollars, accept Bitcoins for payment at the current exchange rate, and then immediately convert those Bitcoins to dollars, never actually holding a Bitcoin.

Security is another concern. Because Bitcoin is essentially digital cash, securing it is vitally important. There is no intermediary that can replace your Bitcoins if they are stolen. As we have seen, however, merchants need not hold Bitcoins, and as interest in Bitcoin expands, we are seeing a great deal of innovation and investment in secure consumer products. But, this still means that exchanges, merchant processors, and other new Bitcoin intermediaries will have to earn consumers' trust just as Visa and PayPal have.

Like the Internet itself, Bitcoin has the potential to be a platform for the kind of permissionless innovation that has driven so much of the growth of our economy. And like all emerging technologies, Bitcoin also presents risks. The challenge for policymakers is to address those risks while doing no harm to the innovative potential of the technology.

Thank you for your time, and I look forward to your questions.

Mr. TIPTON. Thank you, sir.

Our next witness is Adam White, Director of Business Development and Sales at Coinbase. Coinbase is a payment processing company for businesses interested in accepting Bitcoin. Prior to joining Coinbase, Mr. White served in the United States Air Force and was a test pilot for NASA before receiving his MBA from Harvard Business School.

Appreciate you being here with us today, Mr. White, and look forward to your testimony.

STATEMENT OF ADAM WHITE

Mr. WHITE. Thank you, Mr. Chairman, Ranking Member Velázquez, and other members of the Committee, for the opportunity to appear here today.

My name is Adam White. I am the Director of Business Development and Sales at Coinbase, a company founded in June 2012, with the goal of making it easy for merchants and consumers to transact with the digital currency, Bitcoin. More than one million consumers use Coinbase as their digital wallet, and as of today, there are nearly 28,000 businesses that entrust Coinbase to accept Bitcoin payments on their behalf using our payment tools. These merchants include large enterprise-level businesses, such as Overstock.com and Big Fish Games, as well as tens of thousands of small businesses like Tealet, Tuft and Needle, and Mondo Cellars.

Prior to my role at Coinbase, I served as a captain in the United States Air Force, and am a veteran of Operation Iraqi Freedom and Operation Enduring Freedom.

I would like to begin today by outlining the inherent benefits of Bitcoin in commerce, namely the powerful prevention of fraud, the reduction of transaction fees, and the monetization of new markets, and how these benefits could be a positive influence on businesses of all sizes.

Bitcoin enables individuals to push payments to merchants without having to share personally identifiable information that can be intercepted by criminals and used for fraudulent purposes. This irreversible nature of Bitcoin enables the abstraction of personal information and significantly reduces the risk of fraud, something that merchants, card processors, and banks spend billions of dollars per year combatting. With Bitcoin, for example, the target data breach that compromised 40 million consumers' credit card information would not have been possible. Moreover, this irreversibility shields merchants from chargebacks. That is, the forced return of funds from a merchant to a customer's bank account and the cost associated with managing, defending, and preventing fraudulent chargeback claims.

In response, many card issuers and merchants use fraud detection systems that are overly sensitive to trigger activities, especially in card-not-present transactions common online. Initial estimates suggest that some merchants turn away nearly 8 percent if incoming orders due to issues associated with suspicious activity. Many of these transactions, however, are, in fact, legitimate. Bitcoin prevents the need for risk algorithms and ensures merchants capture 100 percent of their customers' orders.

Due to the powerful prevention of fraud and the reduction in the number of intermediaries required to process a payment, Bitcoin transactions are dramatically less expensive than traditional card-based payments. Merchants can reduce their electronic payment acceptance fees to less than 1 percent when accepting payment in Bitcoin. This is especially important for small businesses that sacrifice anywhere between 3 and 5 percent of their revenues in card transaction fees. Businesses can use these savings to reinvest in their company or return them to consumers in the form of lower prices. Moreover, merchants are not subject to a fixed fee per transaction, enabling them to forgo minimum transaction limits and sell small ticket items profitably.

Finally, Bitcoin provides the opportunity to monetize new markets by democratizing foreign exchange and enabling frictionless cross-border transactions that settle immediately. Many products and services are not available for sale in foreign countries because the business cannot manage the payment systems needed to support overseas commerce. Because of the borderless and global nature of Bitcoin, a Bitcoin payment made by a customer in New York looks identical to a merchant, as a Bitcoin payment made by a customer in London, Buenos Aires or Tokyo. There are no individual currency conversion fees associated with Bitcoin payments, so merchants can sell low margin items just as profitably abroad as they do domestically. The ability to easily begin accepting payments from customers around the world can open up whole new markets for merchants and significantly improve topline revenue.

We see Bitcoin as an extremely powerful technology, and it is our goal to bring these efficiencies created by the Bitcoin network to the masses. We are encouraged to see the Committee's proactive examination into the topic of Bitcoin as it relates to small businesses, and I look forward to engaging in dialogue and answering any questions you may have.

Mr. TIPTON. Thank you, Mr. White.

Our next witness is Mark Williams, professor of Finance and Risk at the Boston University School of Management. Before joining the faculty at Boston University, Mr. Williams worked as a senior trading floor executive, bank trust officer and as a bank examiner for the Federal Reserve Bank. Mr. Williams holds an MBA from Boston University School of Business, and a B.S. from the University of Delaware.

Welcome, Mr. Williams, and please begin.

STATEMENT OF MARK WILLIAMS

Mr. WILLIAMS. Thank you. I am very happy to be here, and thank you for inviting me. In particular, I am very interested in Bitcoin, and the reason for that interest really stems from classroom discussions going back to 2011. At that point in time, prices were 35 cents, so it was more of a theoretical discussion, but very quickly within the classroom it moved from discussion to by 2012 when Bitcoin prices started to increase by over a dollar to actually homework assignments, and then eventually, these homework assignments turned into outright discussions and debate in the classroom. By 2013, the price of Bitcoin by January had increased actually to $13 a coin. Very quickly, in 2013, it escalated from $13 all the way up to $1,200. It was remarkable.

But what was unusual about this price run-up at the peak in 2013 was the fact that this was a 9,000 percent increase. Nowhere on this planet or any planet has there been that sort of price increase. And what that represented to the marketplace in particular is the fact that this was a unique product and a unique risk.

So what I would like to do today is I would like to focus specifically not on the promised benefits of Bitcoin, because we have heard enough about that, but I would like to take my discipline in risk management, in particular, working on a commodity trading floor, and talk specifically about the risks that are associated with Bitcoin. In particular, I provided a 30-page testimony which outlines 10 of the specific risks, what I consider to be the top risks associated with Bitcoin. But what I would like to do for the Committee right now is really focus on the top six risks. And I will leave this up for the discussion later.

In particular, the first risk which is very important to look at for big businesses and for little businesses is that Bitcoin itself is not legal tender. And what I mean by that is the fact there is no legal precedence; that is, that individuals and corporations themselves have to accept Bitcoin. So as a result, it is a very voluntary commodity. So just as equally as we can turn a light off today, if the market decides they do not want to accept Bitcoin anymore, the value could drop to worthless. What is very interesting about that statement of worthless, we have seen Bitcoin drop already. Since its high in December, it has dropped by roughly 60 percent. So clearly, this is not a currency. Currencies do not behave like this. But what this is is a high risk speculative commodity.

Since December, what have we seen? We have seen daily price movements of up to 10 percent. Can you imagine having currency in your wallet that can move up or down by 10 percent? That would be hot currency. If you were worried about it dropping by 10 percent, you would be selling it very quickly, getting it out of your wallet. If you thought it would appreciate, you would hoard it. And these characteristics are characteristics that you see in Bitcoin. Over 90 percent of Bitcoin is hoarded. What that means is only 10 percent of what is available trades.

Increasingly, we have had changes within the marketplace. Last week, the IRS came out with a formal ruling and said Bitcoin is not currency. What it is, it is property. And what that means is it reduces the likelihood of people to use it to spend. It actually gives a disincentive. What it increases though is the incentive to hoard. So this is the opposite of what you want in a currency. Currencies, we collectively use currencies because currencies themselves provide us with the ability to buy things. A $100 bill has not value to us to put on the wall, but that $100 bill has value for us to buy art that we can then put on the wall. Bitcoin is unusual in that regard. The fascination, fixation of investors on Bitcoin is tied directly to it as a commodity, as something to speculate, not as something to use as a transactional currency.

So what are some of the other risks? There is extreme price volatility that was discussed earlier as well, and with that extreme price volatility with daily movements of 10 percent, what that means to put it in perspective, Bitcoin is seven times more risky than gold, eight times more risky than the S&P 500. In particular, it is 15 times more risky than the U.S. dollar. And just for fun I will throw this out. If you look at the Argentinian peso, Bitcoin is seven times more risky than the peso.

So as you can see, this is not a currency, but this is a very risky commodity. But more importantly, when we think about businesses, businesses, your average business, they actually have profit margins of maybe 10 percent, 15 to be liberal. If you have a daily fluctuation of 10 percent, what that means is that profit margins can be evaporated within a period of days, and that is of concern.

Two quick more risks that I will bring up to the Committee, and that is the asset bubble. Many noted economists have mentioned this asset bubble, and we have seen it actually since December start to implode. As I mentioned, the price dropped by 60 percent. In addition, the number fifth risk is a growing concentration risk. We are seeing firms like Coinbase doing a nice job of trying to mitigate the market risk, but what is happening is they are moving the risk from let us say 20,000 or 30,000 people to their balance sheet. So they are warehousing that risk and there is not a mature market for them to offload that risk. So we have concentrated risk on their books. They are thinly capitalized. They are a startup. There is no minimum capital requirement. So what should happen if one of these or both of these firms were to blow up? Then consumers, U.S. businesses would be impacted.

And then finally, when we think about Bitcoin, there is Bitcoin tax which now is a risk. In a sense of using Bitcoin on a daily basis, deciding whether to pay, for example, employees or actually accepting it as currency, if you are having daily fluctuations of 10 percent, you can see capital gains very quickly.

So I thank you for your patience.

Mr. TIPTON. Gentlemen, if you would not mind, we apologize. Naturally, when we start, we get a vote called. And we want to make sure that our last witness has the appropriate amount of time and our folks are going to be able to listen. So we will go into recess, run over and vote. I believe it is going to be a short vote. And should be back in 20 minutes or so. Is that about right?

So if you do not mind, I apologize, and certainly appreciate your patience.

[Recess]

Chairman GRAVES. We will go ahead and call the hearing back to order, and I now yield to Ranking Member Velázquez for her introduction.

Ms. VELÁZQUEZ. Thank you, Mr. Chairman.

It is my pleasure to introduce Professor Michael Couvillion. Professor Couvillion is an associate professor of Economics at Plymouth State University's College of Business Administration. His current research includes asset allocation modeling and alternative investment vehicles such as Bitcoin. Additionally, he has worked with the Enterprise Center of Plymouth to educate local, small business owners in New Hampshire about the advantages and disadvantages of Bitcoin.

Welcome, Professor.

STATEMENT OF L. MICHAEL COUVILLION

Mr. COUVILLION. Thank you very much. And thank you to members of the Committee for inviting me.

I thought I would take a slightly different tact this afternoon and not discuss the nuts and bolts of Bitcoin because you have heard so many excellent comments about that before.

My interest in Bitcoin started about three semesters ago when one of my best students wrote a research paper in a class on Bitcoin. He was a passionate advocate for Bitcoin, and he liked it so much he actually put $100 into Bitcoin. He would not tell me how many Bitcoins he bought except that it was well under $10. So the student has graduate and now I keep getting emails from him. "Hey, check out the price of Bitcoin." Because he bought it, I think, about $8, and Bitcoin is worth about $450 right now. So he has got a very nice paper profit here.

So he got me certainly thinking about Bitcoin in a way I had never thought about it before. And I began to become interested in Bitcoin and opened an account with Coinbase in May of last year. I have some data in my written remarks that come from that dataset, which is roughly about 10 months, so it is suggestive, it is recent, but it is by no means definitive.

Some of the things I have learned I would like to share with the Committee. Coinbase charges a different price if you buy Bitcoin than they do if you sell Bitcoin. This is known as the bid-ask spread, very similar to the spreads on a NASDAQ stock let us say in the stock market. And just for a random day, which was March 28th—that is last week—the bid-ask spread for Coinbase was 17 basis points. That is about two-tenths of one percent. By way of comparison, the Dow Jones Industrial Average at the same time had a bid-ask spread of about 45 basis points, twice as high, and the Standard and Poor's 500 had a bid-ask spread of 32 basis points. So on that day, compared to the stock markets, Coinbase's bid-ask spread was lower. In addition, I have taken a look at the trend in the bid-ask spread. The high is 164 basis points, the minimum is zero, and the average is 40. So that is where I got that data you will see on the spreadsheet.

Also, the bid-ask spread has been steadily trending down over time and it is a significant trend. So that is important because bid-ask spreads are an excellent measure of the liquidity of any market. They also have to measure risk because if a market is very thinly traded, you will see much larger bid-ask spreads.

Then, I took a look at the statistics for Bitcoin, asking what kind of distribution does it follow? And my conclusions are that the Bitcoin price return series, that is the percentage daily change, is 2P. It has too many small moves and not enough middling moves. It is also skewed heavily to the right and that causes a problem for using standard or traditional statistical analyses.

Sorry, is my time up? No, okay.

Also, I did a comparison of Bitcoin with three other invesmtents—short-term global interest rates, the dollar index, and the emerging markets currency index, and essentially, I found out that none of those models predict Bitcoin. Its price is in essence unpredictable. You cannot with any degree of accuracy project the price of Bitcoin more than just a few days in the future.

Now, that is good if you are a small businessman, and the reason it is good is that because the average return to Bitcoin is positive—and remember, the price of Bitcoin has risen from about $85 last May to about $450 now. It is a bit seductive to a small business person because if you were to buy Bitcoin, you would see your Bitcoin increase in value. That is only because we have a bullish trend lately. The other thing that you will discover is that the number of daily moves are fewer than they should be at less than 10 percent.

Now, Bitcoin investors, unfortunately, pay for that because while the number of 10 percent or more moves is less than it should be by approximately roughly 2 percent, if you look at the number of 15 percent moves, there are more than there should be. There is about 2 percent of the observations there and huge moves, which we call fat tails, there should be none. In the dataset there were six. Three were positive. Three were negative. But there were six price moves that would be completely unpredictable based on chance. So again, I would like to corroborate what your other witnesses have already told you, that Bitcoin is a very volatile currency.

In terms of the other technical features, the problem with Bitcoin is that we cannot analyze it using the standard tools of finance because the underlying distributions simply does not fit our models. And that means it is hard if you are trying to use sophisticated techniques like value at risk or covariance matrices. It is hard to reach any conclusions that actually work. I realize that small businesses probably will not do that, but even large businesses will have difficulty with Bitcoin for that reason.

I gave a small example of the cost comparison, and Bitcoin works at every level from $1 transactions all the way up to $10,000 transactions. Businesses can save money if they use Bitcoin, and that

I believe is the single fact that is what is going to drive Bitcoin to a successful integration into the marketplace. So there is a slight advantage right there.

Offsetting that, it is difficult for businesses to use Bitcoin because they first have to educate themselves and their employees, and then they have to educate at least some of their customers. And exactly how do you do a trade using Bitcoin? So there is a steep learning curve at first, but once you have managed to get your employees and your customers educated, then things go a whole lot more smoothly. That is a good role here for the government to encourage confident and detailed education on the part of the companies that do a large business in Bitcoin. Because it is so new, you have to educate consumers about that, and because there is so much risk, they also need to be clearly informed and disclosed that this is not an FDIC-insured investment. It is not something that you would ever have invested in before. So I did want to make that point.

Finally, I tried to forecast the price of Bitcoin, and my model suggests that the best predictor of the price of Bitcoin tomorrow is 99 percent of the price today plus $4.73. And that is because there is a positive trend in Bitcoin prices. And I have a graph that shows that basically in 46 days, the price of Bitcoin could be as low as zero or as high as $1,000. That is in 46 days. So it makes it problematic, and I believe that the market for Bitcoin will remain volatile at least for a while unless it achieves mainstream acceptance.

So having said that, there are a couple of advantages of Bitcoin that have not been touched on previously, so I would like to mention them quickly. One is that somehow you can send a message using Bitcoin. There is a way where you could say thank you for your business or some other message like that. I have no idea technically how that happens. I just know that it is possible. So it represents a different way for customers and businesses to communicate with each other. I find that interesting, particularly if you are communicating across the ocean with customers who may be in many, many different parts of the world. That is a benefit there.

The other shoe to drop, so to speak with Bitcoin, is the IRS and its announcement recently that they are going to begin to tax Bitcoin. A lot of people are very, very upset by that in the Bitcoin community because they view it as an announcement that came late.

Chairman GRAVES. Time is expired.

Mr. COUVILLION. Okay, thank you.

Chairman GRAVES. I am now going to turn to questions, and I will let Mr. Hanna open them up.

Mr. HANNA. Thank you.

Mr. Couvillion, you undermine your own argument. The volatility alone proves that it is not a storage of value. Your conversation about the S&P or say pick a stock that is backed by a company with real assets that are in some way attachable, discernible, and measurable because you can go to their website, you can go to their annual reports, there are a thousand ways to figure out what it is you are buying when you buy a company, I find that completely not even relevant. This is about a storage of value that is reliable for people that they can use and go back to that is not volatile. As a matter of fact, any volatility at all that is more than the dollar depreciating over time or some other currency that fluctuates mildly is really, for me, a counterargument.

But I want to ask Mr. Williams, why do we need an imaginary currency? What is there about this that benefits our society or the world at large? And in terms of the underground economy, what are the effects of this—why do we need an imaginary currency in talking about the underground economy?

Mr. WILLIAMS. Great. So let me do it in reverse order, in regard to the underground economy, in particular. This is a potential tool which we have seen already because of Silk Road, to be used in nefarious ways. In essence, there are two aspects of Bitcoin that make it very dangerous in their wrong hands. And the one is the fact that it is anonymous. So that means whoever has it and controls it, owns it. So if you have an account and someone can hack it and grab that coin, not only does that criminal own it, but there is no way to trace down who took it and there is no way from a consumer standpoint to get it back. So in regard to the underground economy, that is one reason why it is a designer currency of choice. Now, it is unfortunate because Silk Road has sort of painted a very negative picture about virtual currencies.

The second aspect of this sort of underworld of virtual currencies is the fact that Bitcoin also is not only anonymous but it is also irreversible. So once that transaction is done, it cannot be pulled back. So let us just say it is transferred by mistake to somebody. There is no way to get that back unless that person is generous and willing to do so. So that is of concern.

Now, the first question you had, excellent question, and that really is what is the benefit? It is questionable in a sense that clearly I view the risks much greater at this point in time than the benefits. In regard to the price volatility, the fact that my colleague to my right can say within 46 days it could be worth zero. Currency is supposed to be used for transactional purposes to facilitate business. If you cannot count on currency, business will not be facilitated. What will happen is that will be hoarded and GDP will drop, employment will drop, and that is a negative thing for business.

So what business needs is confidence in the currency that consumers are going to use. And it is not clear to me that confidence is there with Bitcoin.

Mr. HANNA. Do you want a rebuttal, Mr. Brito?

Mr. BRITO. Thank you. Actually, a couple things.

I think there is a misperception that Bitcoin is completely anonymous. Bitcoin is not completely anonymous. Cash transactions on the other hand are completely anonymous. If I put a bike for sale on Craigslist and I get an email from somebody I do not know, we meet at a park, I give him cash——

Mr. HANNA. But credit cards are not anonymous. I mean, they certainly do not have to be. I can trace them. Checks are not anonymous. And frankly, trading in dollars and not paying your taxes is actually illegal. So, I mean, there is nothing different about Bitcoin than me paying somebody in cash and them not declaring it.

Mr. BRITO. So I was getting to that. Whereas, cash is completely anonymous, credit cards are completely identified. Credit card company knows who I am, who the merchant is, the time, the amount, all of that. Bitcoin is in the middle. It is between cash and credit cards. Because while there is a record captured of every transaction, the amount, we do not know who that is. Now, this is where the Bank Secrecy Act comes in, and companies like Coinbase are required to keep a record of all of their customers. And so, for example, I have an account with Coinbase. They know my name. If there was ever a subpoena related to a particular Bitcoin transaction, Coinbase could turn over my name.

Mr. HANNA. But it requires a subpoena.

Mr. BRITO. The same way with a credit card.

Mr. HANNA. Thank you. Well, right, but credit cards are a lot. I got it.

Thank you, Chairman.

Chairman GRAVES. Ranking Member Velázquez?

Ms. VELÁZQUEZ. Thank you, Mr. Chairman.

Professor Couvillion, last week Iceland announced that it will be releasing a variant of Bitcoin called Auroracoin. This is just one of many other cryptic currencies that exist in addition to Bitcoin. What makes these currencies so different from one another?

Mr. COUVILLION. Thank you for the question.

Bitcoin has what we economists call “first mover advantage,” because it was the first successful digital currency and because it has an overwhelming market share of, I believe, more than 90 percent. It will likely succeed simply because they were there first. There are many, many other different types of currencies, and most of them are variations on the same, but some offer a few different features than Bitcoin does.

Ms. VELÁZQUEZ. Do you think that the market can sustain numerous virtual currencies?

Mr. COUVILLION. No. The parallel I would give is the time in the United States when banks printed their own currency before the Civil War and we saw ultimately the government had to then step in and create a national currency, the dollar. But that is a historical parallel. How good it is, I am not sure.

Ms. VELÁZQUEZ. Okay.

Mr. COUVILLION. However, I do think we will see increasing use of Bitcoin very, very rapidly. I believe it is in the growth phase.

Ms. VELÁZQUEZ. Thank you.

Mr. Williams, in your testimony, you indicate that the Bitcoin financial middlemen, who have multiple business lines, such as Coinbase, have an inherent conflict of interest. Can you please elaborate why you believe that this is the case?

Mr. WILLIAMS. Sure. And that is a correct statement. The inherent conflict of interest with financial middlemen like Coinbase is on one hand they need to mitigate price risks for customers. So what they are interested in doing is being able to once they have the coin, is to sell at the highest price. But Coinbase also has another business line and that is selling Bitcoin to customers. Customers have an interest to buy at the lowest price, so just in those two business lines there is an inherent conflict of interest.

Ms. VELÁZQUEZ. What will regulatory oversight do to protect consumers in these cases?

Mr. WILLIAMS. Right. I would say as regulation seeps into the industry pretty quickly, regulators will look at this and say we have to actually put a wall up with this conflict of interest. It is very significant and it needs to be taken care of.

Ms. VELAZQUEZ. Mr. White, how would you respond to this criticism?

Mr. WHITE. Thank you, Ranking Member Velázquez.

First off, I would say at Coinbase we work very hard to make sure our pricing is completely transparent. So it is important to realize that we offer two prices. We offer a buy price and a sell price, and those are identical for both our merchant services as well as our consumers. So for our consumers that purchase Bitcoins and want to sell those Bitcoins, that is the exact same price that we offer to our merchants. So that bid-ask spread that Mr. Couvillion annotated was about 17 bps, 17 basis points. So we believe it is very small and a fair small price.

There is also in the Bitcoin market, pricing is incredibly transparent. So there are a number of websites out there, one of which is Bitcoincharts.com where you can look at the price of Bitcoin across a number of the largest exchanges or brokerages and determine if whether or not the price you want to pay for a Bitcoin on Coinbase is fair or not. We are held, because of arbitrage, to seek that true price as close as possible.

Ms. VELÁZQUEZ. Okay. Mr. Brito, last week the IRS issued guidance that Bitcoin is to be traded as a property rather than currency for tax purposes. What effect will this have on the Bitcoin and the business ability to accept it as payment?

Mr. BRITO. So, I will begin by saying that I am not a tax professional and you should consult one, but I can say the following. It is going to introduce some accounting headaches because every time that you dispose of a Bitcoin in a transaction, you might be subject to capital gains. What does this do for the person who is accepting it, which is your question? Maybe nothing. If they are a merchant accepting Bitcoins via Coinbase and they choose to never hold Bitcoins, they just take dollars, they really do not have to do anything with that. That is something that consumers or the person who is spending the Bitcoin is going to have to make that accounting.

Now, it is interesting that the choice that the IRS faced was should the coin be treated for tax purposes as currency or as property. And from what I understand, if the choice had been property, it turns out that foreign currencies—sorry, if it had been treated as currency, foreign currency transactions have to account for a gain when you dispose of your foreign currency, just as if it was property. The only difference is that there is a de minimums exemption for currency of $200 per transaction. So in essence, if it had been treated as currency, any transaction under $200, you really did not have to worry about that accounting. We might hope to see that kind of de minimums exemption for property.

Ms. VELAZQUEZ. Mr. Williams, would you care to comment on that question?

Mr. WILLIAMS. Well, I view the blow last week with the IRS as devastating, in particular to Bitcoin. As I mentioned earlier, 90 percent of the coins are hoarded, so in that kind of economy, very few coins circulate. So that is not very liquid. We could look at bid-ask spread. That is only one measurement of liquidity. When we add now the IRS ruling last week, that increases and encourages consumers to horde more, not less. And as a result, that reduces liquidity even more. So it is very concerning. Being the leading financial market in the world, how we view this is extremely important, and it is going to set the tone for other nations as they try to regulate this currency as well.

Ms. VELÁZQUEZ. Thank you. Thank you, Mr. Chairman.

Chairman GRAVES. Mr. Chabot?

Mr. CHABOT. Thank you, Mr. Chairman.

Just a couple questions. In February, CNN Money ran an article regarding the illegal website Silk Road, and it has come up a couple times already in this hearing, and its relationships with Bitcoins. In that they wrote, and I quote, "The Silk Road is primarily used to buy and sell drugs. Bitcoins are the only kind of currency accepted on the site because they are traded electronically and are difficult to trace to individuals," as has also been mentioned. That is a direct quote from the CNN Money Report.

My question is this. If Bitcoin transactions are difficult to trace and also are irreversible, how do we prevent Bitcoins from facilitating criminal activity? And I would open that up to anybody who might like to address it.

Mr. BRITO. So I think, again, by applying the Bank Secrecy Act and your customer rules to Bitcoin intermediaries, and that is something that FinCEN at the Treasury Department has already done and we are seeing these new intermediaries complying with those regulations.

Second, I think it is a question for law enforcement and every time I have spoken to law enforcement, I have heard law enforcement testify, for example, last November's hearing before the Homeland Security Committee, law enforcement has said that they are less concerned about virtual currencies being used for these illicit transactions online than they are about centralized virtual currencies or about cash, indeed. So I think it is a matter of law enforcement doing their job, and they say that they are up to the task, and it is a matter of enforcing our existing money laundering laws.

Mr. CHABOT. Thank you.

Would any of the other members like to address this? Mr. Williams?

Mr. WILLIAMS. Well, I view the anonymous part of Bitcoin as actually being the Achilles heel. The fact it is anonymous, it makes it very dangerous, not only for criminal use for also for consumers. If these coins are stolen by criminals, they cannot be returned.

Mr. CHABOT. Okay. Thank you.

I will go on to another question. Of the number of businesses who sell their services or sell their products online, what percentage would you say—and I know it is difficult to know what it is for sure—but what percentage would you say of the businesses actually accept in some form Bitcoins for their items? Mr. White?

Mr. WHITE. I will take that. So at Coinbase, we have roughly 28,000 merchants that use our payment tools as of today. What is interesting to note is the vast majority, and it is difficult to say with any certainty, but by and large probably 95 percent, if not more, are small businesses. And these are organizations or individuals that are confronted with high credit card fees, issues with chargebacks and financial risk they are just not prepared to handle. And Bitcoin enables them to bypass or avoid a lot of those issues.

Mr. CHABOT. Let me ask you a question. When you say they are small businesses, is there a particular type of small business that they are in general?

Mr. WHITE. Absolutely. So right now what we see is Bitcoin is an incredibly seamless experience when used online. So in line with payment options on a website, it is very simple. Using a Coinbase product, you can click out or you can check out in as simple as two clicks. The vast majority of these businesses are ecommerce facing companies where they sell their products online and accept Bitcoin as a form of payment just with PayPal or credit cards.

Mr. CHABOT. Okay. Now, if you have 28,000 yourself with your company, how many others are out there? What percentage are we talking of the overall businesses on the Internet?

Mr. WHITE. So between Coinbase and our competitors, my best guess would be there is roughly 50,000 businesses that are accepting——

Mr. CHABOT. Altogether you mean?

Mr. WHITE. Altogether here in the U.S. Correct.

Mr. CHABOT. And out of how many are we talking about theoretically? Because I know it is pretty hard to know exactly. Whether it is 50,000 out of——

Mr. WHITE. The vast majority are going to use a Bitcoin payment processor, like Coinbase, because they want to shield themselves.

Mr. CHABOT. I am not asking that. I am asking the 50,000 businesses that are actually utilizing Bitcoin now, out of a universe of how many businesses on the Internet are we talking about? If anybody else might know that——

Mr. BRITO. I imagine it is a very small fraction of businesses, small businesses that accept Bitcoin. I imagine it is less than 1 percent.

Mr. CHABOT. Would you agree with that, Mr. White?

Mr. WHITE. I would agree.

Mr. CHABOT. Less than 1 percent. And you would assume over time—I would assume you would hope that that would grow substantially over time?

Mr. WHITE. We are seeing our merchant services grow at about 10 percent month over month.

Mr. CHABOT. Okay. Are there online gambling businesses that are using this now? And are those any of your folks?

Mr. WHITE. To the best of my knowledge there are. At Coinbase, we do not have the resources to ensure proper compliance with those online gambling organizations, so we do not provide Bitcoin payment processing services for them. But the thing with Bitcoin is you do not necessarily need to use a payment processor like Coinbase. An individual could create an online gambling site and accept Bitcoin directly, but that is not something at Coinbase we support.

Mr. CHABOT. Okay, thank you. I see that my time is ready to expire so I will yield back. Thank you very much.

Chairman GRAVES. Ms. Clarke?

Ms. CLARKE. Thank you very much, Mr. Chairman. And I thank our panelists for coming and sharing their expertise with us today.

My first question is to Mr. Brito. In your written testimony, you mention there is nothing inherent in Bitcoin's design that makes it naturally volatile. You attribute the current volatility to the fact that the currency is new and as such, thinly traded.

My question is twofold. First, how is it that a currency backed by nothing more than market forces, and at the very least, without a central authority to intervene in price destabilization amongst other regulatory issues, that it is not inherently volatile. And then secondly, regarding your explanation on the current volatility, I have gathered from your written testimony that you believe time and increased trading and use will alleviate current volatility. A cynic might suggest that that was an oversimplification at best, or further, assumes that Bitcoin is an asset that can only appreciate, thus forcing stability. How is that unlike any of the previous bubbles we have seen inflate and pop over the course of the past 20 years?

Mr. BRITO. Okay. I appreciate that question.

So in my testimony, I think what I mentioned was that there is nothing inherent in Bitcoin's design that makes it extremely volatile. Extreme volatility. All currencies are volatile, and Bitcoin is certainly a deflationary currency by design. But this extreme volatility that we are seeing probably results from the fact that it is thinly traded. If Bitcoin's economy were to grow and it was much more widely traded, and if we began to see derivative products that allowed you to hedge against Bitcoin's volatility, we should see the volatility subside. Does that mean there would be no volatility? No. Is there a central bank that can intervene and basically introduce more money into the money supply to meet demands? No, there is none of that. So Bitcoin is still going to have a certain amount of volatility, but this extreme volatility is, I guess, what I am addressing.

Does that mean that I see Bitcoin as only ever increasing in value? No. What I am saying is volatility, if Bitcoin's acceptance grows and it begins to be traded more, volatility will subside, but it does not mean that it will subside necessarily in an increasing fashion. It might just reach hopefully a stable range.

Ms. CLARKE. Mr. Williams, did you want to comment on that?

Mr. WILLIAMS. Yes, on a few things.

So since Bitcoin was created in 2009 and started trading, the volatility the first year was 160 percent annualized. That is just unheard of. Since then it has dropped to 140 percent, so we are still in nosebleed territory. That is concerning.

Structurally, there are three reasons why Bitcoin itself is so volatile. The first is the fact that it is hoarded, and that is, as I mentioned earlier, of concern because hoarding allows you to manipulate the price.

The second part, which is very important, is the ownership structure itself is very small. With data that we know so far, at least looking at addresses, not knowing ownerships per se, we know that roughly 29 percent of Bitcoin is owned by 47 people. So you can imagine if 47 people get in a room and say, "Hey, lets not sell," then that sets an artificial floor.

A third thing, which is extremely important, is the fact that when we think about Bitcoin and what is happening here, is not only do we have sort of this scarcity of this commodity, and that is the third point, but it is scarce in a sense that by the year 2140, it maxes at 21 million. So in essence, if you create anything that has a scarcity and you hype up demand and you get enough people that think this is the next new, new thing, then you are going to see prices move and you are going to see high volatility.

So those are the three structural things that have happened, specifically, that I view is why we have seen such extreme volatility. And up until last year, the space rocket went to the moon. This year it is coming back down to earth.

Ms. CLARKE. So the second part to my question was do we see this as a bubble? Would you characterize it is such?

Mr. WILLIAMS. Yes, I would. In December of 2013, I came out very strong adamantly saying that this was a bubble. We have also seen Alan Greenspan on December 4, 2013, come out and say it is a bubble. We saw actually Professor Shiller, a very well-known economist from Yale who came out in January. And it was very interesting the way he described this bubble. He said, "It is not only a bubble, it is an amazing bubble."

More recently, we have also seen additional examples. We know bubbles have three phases—growth, maturity, and pop. And we are clearly seeing the pop phase right now.

Ms. CLARKE. I am out of time, but I thank you gentlemen for your response.

I yield back, Mr. Chairman.

Chairman GRAVES. Mr. Mulvaney?

Mr. MULVANEY. Sure, let us just continue right there.

I guess, Mr. Williams, and this is not where I was going, but just to follow on your last comment, so what? So what if it is a bubble? It is a very small—I mean, this is not like it is the housing bubble. It is not like it is a real estate bubble. It is a very, very small piece of the economy. Right? So what if it is a bubble?

Mr. WILLIAMS. Right. So let us go down that road. So if it is a bubble, then we have these 47 people that are harmed. There is roughly 1,000 people that own roughly 50 percent, so they are harmed. But it does not harm a greater population.

Mr. MULVANEY. Okay.

Mr. WILLIAMS. However, the problem with that logic is the fact that we are talking not about a manufacturer's manufacturing a good; we are talking about currency, which is the lifeblood of economies. We have to rely on currency and trust that currency to have effective business. So in essence, if the currency is flawed, then it impacts negatively our economy.

Mr. MULVANEY. Right. But we just established that it is less than 1 percent of online trade, so, I mean, it is much to do about nothing in terms of the bubble. Right? It might be, it might not be, but I guess in my mind I am hard pressed to see why Congress would care if it is a bubble.

But let us move on to a couple of other things before I get to my own questions.

I had a chance to listen to some of the questions from Mr. Chabot, and my question to you, Mr. Brito, for example, would be Mr. Chabot was clearly concerned about its use, Bitcoin's use in illicit activity, whether it be drug sales, online gambling. Is it technologically possible and practically possible to make Bitcoin say as safe as the dollar when it comes to those types of transactions?

Mr. BRITO. You are asking me if I was a criminal would I rather use a dollar or would I rather use a Bitcoin?

Mr. MULVANEY. I guess so.

Mr. BRITO. And the answer would be no. I mean, I have heard this from numerous law enforcement folks who told me you would be crazy to use a Bitcoin because there is a permanent record made of every Bitcoin transaction. And that is a record that could be accessed years from now to tie you back to a particular transaction. Is it your name? No, it is not your name. It is a pseudonym. It is a Bitcoin address. But there is a permanent record made of that transaction. And what we have seen with Silk Road, which is the example we all know of an online marketplace for drugs that use Bitcoins, is that the FBI successfully took down that website. And today, we are seeing one after another of the vendors on that website being arrested by the FBI.

Mr. MULVANEY. Okay. Thank you.

Let us get to my question then, which is the IRS decision, which Ms. Velá zquez asked I thought some excellent questions about. Start with this, and I will ask everybody to check in on this very quickly because I really do not know where you folk stand on this, was it the right decision? Was the IRS decision to classify this as property and not currency the right decision? We will just go right down the aisle.

Mr. Couvillion, do you want to start? And I will come back. Answer yes or no. We will come back and ask each of you why, but I am trying to get a sense of the panel.

Mr. COUVILLION. No.

Mr. MULVANEY. Okay.

Mr. WILLIAMS. Yes.

Mr. WHITE. I would say no.

Mr. BRITO. Tentative yes.

Mr. MULVANEY. Okay. Here is my question. I guess, because it looks like—which is a nice thing about having a good panel, you get different answers from everybody. It strikes me that it is a way to tax the Internet, is it not? Right now, we do not have taxes on most of the Internet sales, at least we talk about some of them. We are dealing with Main Street fairness and those types of things. It strikes me that this is a way to tax Internet trade. But if I cannot tax the transaction, I will tax the currency that is used to do it. So that is where I am coming from.

Mr. White, you tell me why you think it is no. Mr. Williams, you tell me why you think it is yes.

Mr. WHITE. Yes. So I think what was surprising was the misalignment between the regulators. Right? Because we had FinCEN come out last year and basically describe Bitcoin as a currency. They said companies like Coinbase that operate and provide Bitcoin services, please register as a money service business under FinCEN, and we followed that guidance.

Mr. MULVANEY. You are doing that, right?

Mr. WHITE. We are doing that. Absolutely.

With the IRS's recent guidance that now Bitcoin is a property, there is a mismatch there between how do you exactly describe this asset class? How do you describe Bitcoin? At Coinbase, obviously, we are working with our counsel and working closely with the IRS to seek additional guidance because what we want to do is enable as burdenless as a process as possible for our users to be able to transact in Bitcoin. And right now with this guidance it makes buying a $2 cup of coffee nearly impossible without additional products and services to track that cost basis.

Mr. MULVANEY. Mr. Williams, and maybe the chairman will let you go a little bit more, but if you could give us your answer as to why you think it was the right decision.

Mr. WILLIAMS. Sure. Well, when we look at Bitcoin itself, it is not a currency. To be a currency, it has to be of store value, and see it is not of store value at all. It actually destroys value. Second, we know it is not stable.

Mr. MULVANEY. I am sorry. I have to cut you off. Destroys value? If I bought it at a penny and it is worth $450, does that not create value? I am sorry, what do you mean it destroys value?

Mr. WILLIAMS. Right, so with currency, for example, you want stability. So you want to be able to put it in your wallet and not think about it and then next week use it, not worry about the daily price moving.

Mr. MULVANEY. I have no idea what the name of the currency is in Argentina or in Venezuela. Is it still a currency?

Mr. WILLIAMS. Yes, it is. And earlier I referred to it. Bitcoin is seven times more risky than Argentinian peso.

Mr. MULVANEY. And Venezuela is still a currency? I think you see my point is currency, you go through different phases. But go ahead. Finish your thought.

Mr. WILLIAMS. Okay. So we will move on.

So in regard to another measurement of a strong currency, and that is that it is stable, and we are seeing that there is volatility. So there is not stability in this currency. But most importantly, when we think about a currency, it needs to be liquid, and that is that you can get in and get out. And it is not very clear that you can get in and out at good execution.

But let us move it over. So if it is not currency, what is it? And that is what the IRS is really helping with. In essence, the IRS is saying, okay, well, if it is not currency, what does it look like? Well, if we think about a commodity, right. A commodity is something that is mined. That is Bitcoin. A commodity is something in particular that actually is stored. It is something that is processed. It is something that is resold in the market, and it is something that actually has scarcity. Well, that sounds a lot like Bitcoin. So in essence, I see the IRS ruling as moving more towards commodity. At least it is calling it a product. So I think we are getting closer to the discussion we need to have about what is this.

Mr. MULVANEY. Does Mr. White have a valid point about the misalignment? Why would he have to know his customer if he is dealing in a commodity and not a currency? To you, Mr. Williams. No, does Mr. White have a point? Is he right about the misalignment? One part of this government is treating it as currency and the other is not. He should not have to know his customer if he is only dealing in commodities; right?

Mr. WILLIAMS. Right. So there is a lot of uncertainty about what it is.

Mr. MULVANEY. Right.

Mr. WILLIAMS. And so we saw that with the Treasury Department as it came in last year with this announcement with FinCEN, for example, and how they are working with money transmitters, and we are seeing with the IRS. The picture is getting clearer, but yet there is still a lot of uncertainty out there.

Mr. MULVANEY. Thank you, gentlemen. I appreciate the time. I appreciate the chairman's indulgence in going over a little bit.

Mr. LUETKEMEYER. There we go. Okay, Mr. Payne, five minutes.

Mr. PAYNE. Thank you, Mr. Chairman.

Mr. Mulvaney, the gentleman from South Carolina, was so thorough in his questions, he asked all of mine, so the indulgence for additional time probably cost me my questions. So I yield back.

Mr. LUETKEMEYER. Mr. Payne, if you can think of anything in the meantime, let us know. I will be happy to get back to you. As we go through the discussions, a lot of times questions pop up and we want to make sure you have an opportunity to ask anything that may come up. But I understand. I was sitting here and I checked off all my questions. They were being asked as well.

With that, Mr. Schweikert, you are up next. You have five minutes.

Mr. SCHWEIKERT. Thank you, Mr. Chairman. And Mr. Payne just proved he is actually the smartest member of the Committee because brevity I think is a sign of being brilliant. And now I am going to break that.

Okay. I want to actually sort of back up a little bit and have a conversation that is a little less transactional. And I do not mean to move almost ethereal. I sat on actually Monetary Policy a couple years ago, and I think we were one of the first meeting where part of it went off and we had the discussion of alternative currencies. And I almost am uncomfortable using the term alternative currency and more alternative units of value or acceptance and trade.

What else is on the horizon? You know, Bitcoin appeared, what 2009? What else is out there? What other alternative exchanges of value do you see coming that are going to take advantage of the Internet universe? Because you and I can is there and come up if we really think it through, you know, tokens in a babysitting exchange are ultimately units of value in exchange. I mean, this is not—conceptually, it is not new. But with technology, what is next on the horizon?

Mr. BRITO. So I think one thing that we have been doing here is focusing so much about Bitcoin being currency or being money, and I think that misses the point. Currency or money has three properties. Right? It is a medium of exchange, a store value, and it is a unit of account. Now, Bitcoin probably is not good at all of those three, certainly not right now. As Mr. Williams so eloquently put forth, it is not a good unit of account. I certainly would not want my mortgage or my salary denominated in Bitcoin, and it is not a good store value because of its volatility. But what about medium of exchange? Is it a good medium of exchange? And I think with the 50,000 merchants, usually all small businesses that are accepting Bitcoin today, are telling us that this is a very good medium of exchange.

Mr. SCHWEIKERT. My question was what is next on the horizon?

Mr. BRITO. Okay. So jumping from there.

Mr. SCHWEIKERT. Is there Bitcoin 2? Is there someone that is going to take a million bucks of gold and say I am going to produce an electronic currency that has a gold peg? What else is next?

Mr. BRITO. So I think the next thing we are going to see is that because Bitcoin at base is simply a ledger that keeps track of value being transacted, there is no reason why a Bitcoin has to represent only a dollar. A Bitcoin could also represent anything else. An ounce of gold, a share of stock, a car.

Mr. SCHWEIKERT. So you could see a generation——

Mr. BRITO. Commodities markets based on Bitcoins.

Mr. SCHWEIKERT. I want to bounce to Mr. White. The question, what is next on the horizon?

Mr. WHITE. That is a great question. We see Bitcoin as more than just a payment network in digital currency. This is the first application of Bitcoin as the protocol. The core technological problem that was solved here has never been solved before, and that is the ability to prove and transfer ownership without the need of a trusted third party.

Mr. SCHWEIKERT. Okay. So is there the next generation on the horizon?

Mr. WHITE. Exactly. So Mr. Brito said that you can attach this one satoshi, the smallest amount of a Bitcoin worth much less than a fraction of a penny to an asset or a stock. So in essence, you could provide this ability to trade assets. You could also use it as a date timestamp to prove ownership of an idea using the blockchain, which is this universally distributed ledger that no one central body controls.

Mr. SCHWEIKERT. Okay. Mr. Williams, that sort of concept, what is next on the horizon in this concept?

Mr. WILLIAMS. Well, if you open the door and you call it a currency, then that is a real slippery slope.

Mr. SCHWEIKERT. You know of my preference of value of exchange.

Mr. WILLIAMS. Okay. So if we slam that door shut, then it is not a nationless currency. Then you have more control. And then what is it? Well, it is a payment system. How is it different than ACH? And the question is, well, it is definitely much more sophisticated. ACH happened. This payment system in the 1970s, the Fed had a lot of influence over that system, but it still remains to be an efficient system. So all of a sudden you have focus now on the payment benefits of Bitcoin, and then you have competition within that payment system. And we have a discussion no longer about currency.

Mr. SCHWEIKERT. Do you see something else on the horizon that takes this technology that goes to the next level?

Mr. WILLIAMS. Right. So then——

Mr. SCHWEIKERT. Or a commodity pegged to such electronic currency or something else?

Mr. WILLIAMS. Right. So yes, I do. What we will see is more asset classes that can be pushed through this payment system.

Mr. SCHWEIKERT. Okay. And Mr. Couvillion, and my mother's maiden name, please, the same question. What else is next on the horizon?

Mr. COUVILLION. In terms of the next thing on the horizon that I think the Committee might be interested in taking a look at, there are at least three serious proposals to get approval to launch Bitcoin-based exchange traded funds, commonly called ETFs, such as the diamonds, the spiders, the NASDAQ cubes. There are more than 400 others. If they do get approval to launch these Bitcoin ETFs, it may be possible by the end of this year, if you have a self-directed IRA, to put in effect Bitcoin into your individual retirement.

Mr. SCHWEIKERT. Or hold a Bitcoin denominated?

Mr. COUVILLION. Exactly.

Mr. SCHWEIKERT. In other words, you would look at it just in the reverse.

Mr. COUVILLION. Exactly. And I am not sure that that is a wise idea.

Mr. SCHWEIKERT. Mr. Chairman, I know I am a little over time, but there is a fascinating philosophical debate underlying here for those of you who are followers of sort of monetary policy. Mr. Williams just spoke, a nationless currency or value of exchange. I am not sure that is a bad thing. And in many ways we have had it forever. I mean, a gold peg contract. But also something of Bitcoin, yes, it is a challenge to being a reserve currency but the benefits we gain as a country being the reserve currency is we have minimal transaction costs; correct?

Mr. COUVILLION. Yes.

Mr. SCHWEIKERT. And if all of a sudden there is another medium of exchange that no longer has that transaction cost spiff benefit, it also becomes a threat to becoming the reserve currency.

Let us start with Mr. Williams, just because you and I seem to be the farthest outliers from each other. Tell me where I am wrong on both those premises.

Mr. WILLIAMS. Well, you say what is wrong with a nationless currency. So we are back—you opened that door that we shut I thought earlier, and that was it cannot be a currency.

Mr. SCHWEIKERT. Then that is why we were—Mr. Williams, that is why we were reusing the term "value of exchange"; correct?

Mr. WILLIAMS. All right. So now if this is a value of exchange, then it will not compete with nation currency, such as the U.S. dollar.

E: Well, the fact of the matter is any type of exchange, whether I am willing to exchange diamonds or gold or anything else, ultimately is—has inflationary, disinflationary effects on exchanges of value and commodities and other things.

So, and first, let us go through my couple of questions. Let us try these.

Threat to reserve currency if it becomes an efficient means of avoiding the exchange cost. Yes? No?

Mr. WILLIAMS. I do not view it as a threat because of this high volatility that we see.

Mr. SCHWEIKERT. Okay. But if you and I are sitting here a decade from now and there is ETFs and others, assuming this concept even survives that long, that volatility would ultimately be squeezed away because of the amount of participation. Because would you agree that much of the volatility today is because of how thin the market is?

Mr. WILLIAMS. Right. So I would disagree with that. There is structural problems and it has less to do with the fact of how thinly it is traded. It is actually how it is structured.

So good question though in regard to looking forward what could happen. A competition within currencies. That is what we have in the global financial markets. Sometimes the dollar is stronger, sometimes it is weaker against other currencies. So if this could ever gain that status, then it would be in the mix and be competitive.

Mr. SCHWEIKERT. But what becomes fascinating there in monetary policy is all of a sudden you would have a currency without intervention from a central bank which becomes a fascinating—you actually have an honest peg of value compared to—let us be completely honest—pegs of value of currency, nation currency that do have a certain level of intervention, and therefore, manipulation.

Mr. WILLIAMS. So I am going to stir it up a little bit. I have made this statement before. So with the U.S. dollar, we have central bankers in the monetary policy you have spoken about and they determine how much of the money supply increases or decreases to spur economic growth for our businesses. If we go to a Bitcoin-type currency, then the new central bankers is the computer program itself and those miners that mine it. So the question is not that central bankers go away but they just are different people.

Mr. SCHWEIKERT. Yeah. And now you are heading in the direction I was hoping to have the conversation. I am sorry. I told you it was going to get slightly ethereal.

Do we let—Mr. Brito——

Mr. BRITO. Yes.

Mr. SCHWEIKERT.—had one comment and then I thank you. You have been very patient with my ramblings.

Mr. BRITO. I will simply say that this is something that Milton Friedman proposed that we should replace humans at a board determining the money supply with a computer that had a set of rules and simply determined the money supply based on the algorithm. The thing about Milton Friedman's proposal is that the computer, you can always go in and reprogram it. A human could always go in and reprogram it with a currency like Bitcoin or another currency. Once you set the algorithm in place and you have a wide diversity of miners and others running that program, it becomes virtually impossible to change. That algorithm change the money supply.

Mr. SCHWEIKERT. Mr. Chairman, I am one that believes by the end of this decade I will see another type of alternative value of exchange here, but will we have some collective or others that attach some reserve value or a peg of value or something of that which may deal with the stability issue, but it does actually start to become both a threat to a country like ours where we carry a large deficit and we use certain monetary policy, inflationary policies and others to be able to value back those future payments. But in many ways you are seeing I think the tip of an iceberg of a fascinating discussion.

Thank you, Mr. Chairman.

Mr. TIPTON. As you can see, Mr. Schweikert is a very, very thoughtful member of our Committee.

Let us go for round two. If anybody has any extra questions, we will go through those. We will start with Ms. Clarke.

Ms. CLARKE. Thank you, Mr. Chairman. I do have one final question for Mr. Brito.

Mr. Brito, you mentioned that one-quarter of Americans who are unbanked and underbanked could look to Bitcoin as an important new option, and a good number of these unbanked and underbanked individuals are one step away from absolute financial calamity. How would Bitcoin be an effective buttress against the calamity given its valuation swings?

Mr. BRITO. So I said it could potentially be seen as a new option for the unbanked and the underbanked. So the unbanked and the underbanked traditionally, they do not have bank accounts. They do not have credit cards. They use Payday loans. They have to buy prepaid cards. With something like Bitcoin, it allows for them to have electronic transactions and perhaps at a much cheaper cost. Right? So if you are going to a merchant that is giving you a discount because you are using Bitcoin, you can do that.

Is that going to happen tomorrow? No, I do not think that is going to happen tomorrow. But the beauty of Bitcoin is it is an experiment and its potential is huge. So I think what we need to do is allow the experiment to go on. Today, state regulators are coming up with regulations that are consumer protection regulations and make sure the Bitcoin businesses are well capitalized, comply with disclosure, et cetera, et cetera. We need to make sure that those rules are consistent and clear so that we can have these products potentially become available to these consumers. Is it available today? No. But if we take the view that the risks just outweigh the benefits at all points, and we should not even think about this thing, then we are going to—in order to avoid the risks, you are going to give up all the potential benefits, and that would be a real shame.

Ms. CLARKE. Thank you, Mr. Brito. Thank you, Mr. Chairman. Thank the panelists today. I yield back.

Mr. TIPTON. Thank you.

Mr. Mulvaney, do you have any second questions?

Mr. MULVANEY. Sure, real briefly.

Continue there, Mr. Brito. In terms of allowing this experiment to run its course, how damaging is the IRS decision?

Mr. BRITO. So earlier you asked me if I thought the IRS decision was right or wrong, and I said tentatively yes. Let me tell you why. The IRS only had a choice between designating it a currency or property. Those were its two choices given to it by Congress. And so between those two, I think Mr. Williams is right, technically it looked at the thing and it looks more like property. So technically, they probably made the correct decision that was available to it.

Now, it does create this problem that Mr. White was alluding to, where potentially now if you want to buy a cup of coffee you have to calculate your capital gains. Some folks think it should have been treated as a currency because if it were currency, then there is a $200 de minimums exemption. Right? So if you are buying something under $200, you do not have to worry about capital gains. Perhaps it is something that Congress should consider having that kind of exemption for property or perhaps creating a new category for virtual currencies to allow the kind of entrepreneurship and development that might get these products out to the world.

Mr. MULVANEY. My staffers mentioned something, again, I know a little bit about Bitcoin, mostly on account of the presentation you made to the Monetary Policy and Trade Subcommittee on Financial Services. But I do not know that much about it. My staffers are telling that Germany has classified it in a very special way as a private currency. Is that an option that might be available to us? Is that something that makes sense?

Mr. BRITO. So I am not a tax expert, as I mentioned before, so I am not 100 percent on that. I could look into that.

Mr. MULVANEY. Mr. Williams, are you familiar with that at all? No?

Mr. WILLIAMS. No. I am not a tax expert either.

Mr. MULVANEY. Gotcha. And again, Mr. Chairman, so what I am hearing is it is classified as something else in other countries, so maybe Mr. Brito is onto something that it is not currency and it is not property. It is something new. Perhaps not too surprising in this 21st century that we have new types of things. So it is something we will take a look at.

Thank you, gentlemen, very much. It is very enlightening.

Mr. LUETKEMEYER. Yes, Mr. Couvillion, you have a comment?

Mr. COUVILLION. Yes, I do. I would like to read a very short statement from Alistair Nevius, who is the Journal of Accountancy's editor-in-chief for tax matters.

"The IRS warns that taxpayers who treated virtual currencies inconsistently with the notice before the date the notice was issued will not get penalty relief unless they can establish that their underpayment or failure to properly file information returns was due to reasonable cause. Many people believe that because the IRS announcement came out three weeks before income tax forms are due and because many taxpayers have already filed their income tax returns, everyone, at least for this year, should be able to use the reasonable cause."

Mr. MULVANEY. Mr. Chairman, if I may, Mr. Couvillion, if I may interrupt, there is no way to do that, is there? What you have just read to us says the IRS expects you to treat it—to have been treating it as property from the beginning of time and that if you filed, I guess, last year or if you have already filed this year, they expect you to pay taxes on it as if it was property. Does small business have the ability to do that? Have they been tracking it as property this whole time or have they been treating it as currency?

Mr. COUVILLION. It can be done. You can go back and audit, but it is not something anybody thought we would ever have to do two years ago, three years ago, and so it creates a huge paperwork burden. Technology can help, but especially this year, many people think it is simply unfair to expect taxpayers to amend their returns at this late date because the IRS just issued this ruling.

Mr. LUETKEMEYER. Mr. Brito, not to interrupt, did you not mention a while ago that every single Bitcoin transaction is documented so that there would be the ability then, even to buy a cup of coffee, be able to go back and recreate a record for an individual's transactions over the course of a year to see whether they gained or lost or whatever?

Mr. BRITO. Sure. And I also think that the tax consequences for this year for consumers, or at least I should say the compliance costs are not going to be huge simply because most—the folks who are today holding and spending Bitcoins, it is not your grandma. It is not your average Joe. It is people who know what they are investing in, what they are doing. And they have known that there was going to be a tax—an IRS guidance coming out soon. And so they have probably filed for extensions, so they are not filing on April 15th. They are probably doing that in September. And even if that is the case, the IRS is probably not going to audit you for very small transactions. It is going to be if you have—if you are not declaring capital gains on $20,000 worth of Bitcoin.

Mr. TIPTON. The rules document the database of transactions.

Mr. BRITO. The transactions, it is available to anyone. It is online. You can download it. Anybody can download it at any moment.

Mr. TIPTON. So the IRS has full access to this document or this database?

Mr. BRITO. This database. Yes.

Mr. TIPTON. Okay.

Mr. Mulvaney, do you have any other follow ups?

Ms. Herrera, would you like to ask any questions?

Okay. I do not have very many. I just have one or two. With regards to hedging Bitcoins, you mentioned a while ago, Mr. Brito, they do not do that yet. Is that correct?

Mr. BRITO. So there are no—to my knowledge, there are no options or exchange traded futures or options available on Bitcoin. There are some companies today, some exchanges today that are looking to get CFTC approval to offer those. But I think Mr. White probably could speak more to how Coinbase might be hedging.

Mr. LUETKEMEYER. So if they are looking to start hedging, would that make it a currency then or would that make it a commodity?

Mr. BRITO. I do not think the fact that you are hedging against a value of something, that alone does not speak to whether it is a commodity or currency.

Mr. LUETKEMEYER. Okay. Very good. I have no other further questions. I certainly enjoyed the conversation here. It is certainly thought-provoking to see something like this. I think Mr. Schweikert is kind of also on the cusp here of some things. Is this today's currency and 10 years from now there is going to be another Bitcoin 2 or some other entity out there, whatever it is called, that will be a new method of transfer of payment. You know, who knows? I think as our economies continue to evolve and trade continues to take place, people are going to find ways to trade. From the beginning of time we have been bartering and trading. And so today's world is no different. We just use currency right now as a traditional way of transacting trades, but that being said, I come from rural Missouri. There is still a lot of bartering that goes on where I live. You trade this for that and the IRS never knows anything about it.

So with that, as we close the hearing, I would like to again thank all the witnesses for being here and thank you for sharing your expertise, both with the members of this Committee and the small business community. I believe that today's discussion provides valuable information about the benefits and risks associated with Bitcoin and other virtual currencies as the government further examines this alternative payment system.

With that, I ask unanimous consent that members have five legislative days to submit statements and supporting materials for the record.

Without objection, so ordered.

This hearing is now adjourned. Thank you very much.

[Whereupon, at 3:08 p.m., the Committee was adjourned.]

APPENDIX

MERCATUS CENTER
George Mason University
Bridging the gap between academic ideas and real-world problems

TESTIMONY

BENEFITS AND RISKS OF BITCOIN FOR SMALL BUSINESSES

JERRY BRITO
Senior Research Fellow, Mercatus Center at George Mason University

House Committee on Small Business
April 2, 2014

Mr. Chairman and members of the committee, thank you for inviting me here today to comment on Bitcoin's use for small businesses. My name is Jerry Brito and I am a senior research fellow at the Mercatus Center at George Mason University, where I study the regulation of emerging technologies in the Mercatus Center's Technology Policy Program.

INTRODUCTION

Online virtual currencies are nothing new. They have existed for decades—from World of Warcraft Gold to Facebook Credits to e-gold. Neither are online payments systems new. PayPal, Visa, and Western Union Pay are all examples. So what is it about Bitcoin that makes it unique?

- Bitcoin is the world's first completely decentralized digital currency.
- Its decentralized nature results in lower transactions costs, making it particularly attractive to small businesses.
- It could also be an attractive electronic payments option for consumers, including the unbanked and underbanked.
- Risks include volatility and security, but these are not problems inherent in Bitcoin's design.

The policy challenge is to address the risks associated with Bitcoin without stifling innovation.

BACKGROUND

Whatever one may think about Bitcoin's prospects for enduring value, it is safe to say that it is a remarkable technical achievement.[1] Bitcoin is the world's first completely decentralized digital currency, and it's the decentral-

1. The attached appendix is an updated version of *Bitcoin: A Primer for Policymakers* by me and Andrea Castillo, which goes into considerable detail about the technical workings of Bitcoin, as well as a detailed description of the cryptocurrency's potential benefits not just for consumers

For more information or to meet with the scholar, contact
Taylor Barkley, (703) 993-8205, tbarkley@mercatus.gmu.edu
Mercatus Center at George Mason University, 3434 Washington Boulevard, 4th Floor, Arlington, VA 22201

ized part that makes it unique. Prior to Bitcoin's invention in 2009, online currencies or payments systems had to be managed by a central authority, whether it was Facebook issuing Facebook Credits or PayPal ensuring that transactions between its customers were reconciled. However, by solving a longstanding conundrum in computer science known as the "double spend" problem, Bitcoin for the first time makes possible transactions online that are person to person, without the need for an intermediary between them, just like cash.

BENEFITS

This technical breakthrough presents both potential benefits and risks for consumers and small businesses.

For example, because there is no central intermediary in Bitcoin transactions, fees associated with those transactions are relatively small. Small businesses accepting credit card payments often face fees of around 25 cents for each card swipe, plus two to four percent of the transaction total. If you are a small-margin business, those fees can really eat into your bottom line. This is why we often see small businesses like dry cleaners or convenience stores display signs limiting credit cards to transactions over a certain amount. In contrast, businesses that use a merchant processor like BitPay or Coinbase pay fees of one percent or less on Bitcoin transactions. If you are a small-margin business, that difference could mean doubling your profits.

Another reason small businesses are attracted to Bitcoin is that, like cash, all transactions are final. Again, because there is no central intermediary, there is no third party that can reverse a transaction. This protects small businesses from chargeback fraud, which often results not just in the loss of the sale, but also in penalty fees. Such "friendly fraud" accounts for 41 percent of all claims,[2] and if a merchant has one percent of their charges reversed as chargebacks, they can be kicked out of the credit card networks, potentially ending their business.[3]

Finally, because Bitcoin is decentralized, businesses can now accept international payments that were not previously possible. There are over 50 countries that traditional payment processors do not serve, often because of high fraud rates.[4] Because Bitcoin payments are global and final, doing business with consumers in those countries is now feasible. For example, one small electronics retailer who accepts Bitcoin payments recently noted that over the last nine months he sold $300,000 worth of merchandise to nearly 40 countries.[5] This includes countries like Pakistan and Moldova, which were previously unavailable to American merchants. "We could never ship to these countries using a system other than Bitcoin," he wrote.

For consumers, the benefit Bitcoin presents is essentially choice. Wishing to encourage its use, merchants frequently offer discounts to customers who pay with Bitcoin. Now consumers can choose to pay a little more and get the benefits of using a credit card, like fraud insurance and airline miles, or pay a little less. For some price-sensitive consumers, this could be a very valuable choice. More than a quarter of American households are either unbanked or underbanked, and many rely on prepaid cards for access to electronic payments.[6] Bitcoin could potentially be an important new option for these consumers.

---

and the economy, but also for free speech and oppressed minorities around the world. It also looks at Bitcoin's challenges, including the currency's security and volatility, as well as law enforcement concerns and regulatory alternatives.

2. CyberSource, 2012 Online Fraud Report, http://tinyurl.com/n3ze9pw.
3. Elizabeth Harper, "Friendly Fraud? Yes It Exists," *Christian Science Monitor* (blog), March 11, 2014, http://www.csmonitor.com/Business/Saving-Money/2014/0311/Friendly-fraud-Yes-it-exists.
4. Andy Skelton, "Pay Another Way: Bitcoin," *WordPress* (blog), November 15, 2012, http://en.blog.wordpress.com/2012/11/15/pay-another-way-bitcoin/.
5. Dylan Love, "A Guy Who Owns a Bitcoin-Only Electronics Store Is Revealing Everything on Reddit," *Business Insider*, March 18, 2014, http://www.businessinsider.com/e-commerce-with-bitcoin-2014-3.
6. FDIC, *2011 FDIC National Survey of Unbanked And Underbanked Households*, September 2012, https://www.fdic.gov/householdsurvey/2012_unbankedreport.pdf.

RISKS

Of course, there are also risks associated with Bitcoin. Chief among these is Bitcoin's historic volatility. It has traded from a low of pennies when it was first introduced in 2009 to a high of $1,200 last December, with wild short-term swings. However, there is nothing inherent in Bitcoin's design that makes it naturally volatile. Its volatility is likely attributable to the fact that it is a new currency, still in the process of discovering its stable price. Additionally, as a nascent currency, it is very thinly traded and as a result a single large-enough trade can affect the exchange price substantially. If Bitcoin's use continues to expand, we should expect to see volatility subside. Additionally, derivatives that allow investors to bet against the price of Bitcoin will soon become available, and this should help stabilize the price as well.[7]

It should also be noted that small businesses can use Bitcoin entirely as a payment system, and in fact, this is what most do. Using a merchant service company like BitPay or Coinbase, they do not need to be exposed to Bitcoin volatility. Merchants can denominate prices in dollars, accept bitcoins for payment at the current exchange rate, and then immediately convert those bitcoins to dollars. Indeed, a business that accepts Bitcoin payments never has to hold bitcoins.

Security is another concern. Because Bitcoin is essentially digital cash, securing it is vitally important. There is no intermediary that can replace your bitcoins if they are stolen. As we have seen, however, merchants need not hold bitcoins, and as interest in Bitcoin expands we are seeing a great deal of innovation and investment in secure consumer products.

Like the Internet itself, Bitcoin has the potential to be a platform for the kind of permissionless innovation that has driven so much of the growth of our economy.[8] And like all emerging technologies, Bitcoin also presents risks. The challenge for policymakers is to address those risks while doing no harm to the innovative potential of the technology.

Thank you for your time and I look forward to your questions.

ABOUT THE AUTHOR

Jerry Brito is a senior research fellow at the Mercatus Center at George Mason University and director of its Technology Policy Program. He also serves as an adjunct professor of law at George Mason University. His research focuses on technology and Internet policy, copyright, and the regulatory process.

ABOUT THE MERCATUS CENTER

7. Katy Burne, "New Derivative Guards Against Bitcoin's Price Swings," *Wall Street Journal*, March 24, 2014, http://blogs.wsj.com/moneybeat/2014/03/24/new-derivative-guards-against-bitcoins-price-swings/.
8. See Adam Thierer, *Permissionless Innovation: The Continuing Case for Comprehensive Technological Freedom* (Arlington, VA: Mercatus Center at George Mason University, 2014), http://permissionlessinnovation.org.

APPENDIX

Bitcoin: A Primer for Policymakers

Jerry Brito[1]
Andrea Castillo[2]

Bitcoin is the world's first completely decentralized digital currency. Four short years ago, knowledge of it was confined to a handful of hobbyists on Internet forums. Today, the bitcoin economy is larger than the economies of some of the world's smaller nations. The value of a bitcoin (or BTC) has grown and fluctuated greatly, from pennies in its early days to over $390 at its peak in November 2013. The current market capitalization of the bitcoin economy is estimated to be over $4 billion.[3] Businesses big and small have shown interest in integrating the Bitcoin platform into their operations and providing new services within the bitcoin economy. Venture capitalists, too, are eager to put their money behind this growing industry.[4] Traditional financial institutions and researchers, too, have taken notice. Noting its rapid development and status as a "remarkable conceptual and technical achievement," the Federal Reserve Bank of Chicago recently released a primer on the cryptocurrency.[5] The development of Bitcoin and its early successes are an exciting testament to the ingenuity of the modern entrepreneur.

Because Bitcoin is decentralized, it can be used pseudonymously, and this has attracted the attention of regulators. The same qualities that make Bitcoin attractive as a payment system could also allow users to evade taxes, launder money, and trade illicit goods. Both the Financial Crimes Enforcement Network (FinCEN) of the US Department of the Treasury[6] and the Department of Justice[7] have released official statements regarding the regulation of virtual currencies, including Bitcoin. A Government Accountability Office report on virtual currencies urged the IRS to reduce tax-compliance risks by issuing a guidance.[8] The appendix of that report contains a letter from IRS Deputy Commissioner Steven T. Miller, who assured the office that the IRS is "working to address these risks." Additionally, a commissioner of the Commodities Futures Trading Commission recently expressed interest in exploring whether Bitcoin falls

---

[1] Jerry Brito is a senior research fellow at the Mercatus Center at George Mason University.
[2] Andrea Castillo is a research assistant at the Mercatus Center at George Mason University.
[3] Financial information provided at bitcoincharts.com estimates total market capitalization to be $4,097,390,850 as of November 12, 2013.
[4] Sarah E. Needleman and Spencer E. Ante, "Bitcoin Startups Begin to Attract Real Cash," *Wall Street Journal*, May 8, 2013, http://online.wsj.com/article/SB10001424127887323687604578469012375269952.html.
[5] François R. Velde, "Bitcoin: A Primer," *Essays On Issues*, Number 317, Federal Reserve Bank of Chicago, December 2013, http://www.chicagofed.org/digital_assets/publications/chicago_fed_letter/2013/cfldecember2013_317.pdf.
[6] US Department of the Treasury, Financial Crimes and Enforcement Network, "Application of FinCEN's Regulations to Persons Administering, Exchanging, or Using Virtual Currencies" (Regulatory Guidance, FIN-2013-G001, US Department of the Treasury, Washington, DC, March 18, 2013), http://fincen.gov/statutes_regs/guidance/html/FIN-2013-G001.html.
[7] Jennifer Shasky Calvery, "Combating Transnational Organized Crime: International Money Laundering as a Threat to Our Financial Systems" (Statement for the Record Before the Subcommittee on Crime, Terrorism, and Homeland Security of the House Committee on the Judiciary, February 8, 2012), http://www.justice.gov/ola/testimony/112-2/02-08-12-crm-shasky-calvery-testimony.pdf.
[8] US Government Accountability Office, "Virtual Economies and Currencies: Additional IRS Guidance Could Reduce Compliance Risks" (report to the Senate Committee on Finance, GAO-13-516, May, 2013), http://www.gao.gov/assets/660/654620.pdf.

within the commission's jurisdiction.[9] In considering how to best oversee this still-nascent technology, government regulators should take care that their overlapping directives do not hinder the promising growth potential of this innovative financial platform.

This paper will provide a short introduction to the Bitcoin network, including its properties, operations, and pseudonymous character. It will describe the benefits of allowing the Bitcoin network to develop and innovate, while highlighting issues of concern for consumers, policymakers, and regulators. It will describe the current regulatory landscape and explore other potential regulations that could be promulgated. The paper will conclude by providing policy recommendations that will assuage policymakers' common concerns while allowing for innovation within the Bitcoin network.

What Is Bitcoin?

Bitcoin is an open-source, peer-to-peer digital currency. Among many other things, what makes Bitcoin unique is that it is the world's first completely decentralized digital-payments system. This may sound complicated, but the underlying concepts are not difficult to understand.

Overview

Until Bitcoin's invention in 2008 by the unidentified programmer known as Satoshi Nakamoto, online transactions always required a trusted third-party intermediary. For example, if Alice wanted to send $100 to Bob over the Internet, she would have had to rely on a third-party service like PayPal or MasterCard. Intermediaries like PayPal keep a ledger of account holders' balances. When Alice sends Bob $100, PayPal deducts the amount from her account and adds it to Bob's account.

Without such intermediaries, digital money could be spent twice. Imagine there are no intermediaries with ledgers, and digital cash is simply a computer file, just as digital documents are computer files. Alice could send $100 to Bob by attaching a money file to a message. But just as with email, sending an attachment does not remove it from one's computer. Alice would retain a copy of the money file after she had sent it. She could then easily send the *same* $100 to Charlie. In computer science, this is known as the "double-spending" problem,[10] and until Bitcoin it could only be solved by employing a ledger-keeping trusted third party.

Bitcoin's invention is revolutionary because for the first time the double-spending problem can be solved without the need for a third party. Bitcoin does this by distributing the necessary ledger among all the users of the system via a peer-to-peer network. Every transaction that occurs in the bitcoin economy is registered in a public, distributed ledger, which is called the block chain. New transactions are checked against the block chain to ensure that the same bitcoins haven't been previously spent, thus eliminating the double-spending problem. The global peer-to-peer network, composed of thousands of users, takes the place of an intermediary; Alice and Bob can transact without PayPal.

One thing to note right away is that transactions on the Bitcoin network are not denominated in dollars or euros or yen as they are on PayPal, but are instead denominated in bitcoins. This makes it a virtual currency in addition to a decentralized payments network. The value of the currency is not derived from gold or government fiat, but from the value that people assign to it.

---

[9] Tracy Alloway, Gregory Meyer, and Stephen Foley, "US Regulators Eye Bitcoin Supervision," *Financial Times*, May 6, 2013, http://www.ft.com/intl/cms/s/0/b810157c-b651-11e2-93ba-00144feabdc0.html.
[10] David Chaum, "Achieving Electronic Privacy," *Scientific American*, August 1992, 96–101.

The dollar value of a bitcoin is determined on an open market, just as is the exchange rate between different world currencies.[11]

Operation

So far we have discussed what Bitcoin is: a decentralized peer-to-peer payments network and a virtual currency that essentially operates as online cash. Now we will take a closer look at how Bitcoin works.

Transactions are verified, and double-spending is prevented, through the clever use of public-key cryptography.[12] Public-key cryptography requires that each user be assigned two "keys," one private key that is kept secret like a password, and one public key that can be shared with the world. When Alice decides to transfer bitcoins to Bob, she creates a message, called a "transaction," which contains Bob's public key, and she "signs" it with her private key. By looking at Alice's public key, anyone can verify that the transaction was indeed signed with her private key, that it is an authentic exchange, and that Bob is the new owner of the funds. The transaction—and thus the transfer of ownership of the bitcoins—is recorded, time-stamped, and displayed in one "block" of the block chain. Public-key cryptography ensures that all computers in the network have a constantly updated and *verified* record of all transactions within the Bitcoin network, which prevents double-spending and fraud.

What does it mean when we say that "the network" verifies transactions and reconciles the ledger? And how exactly are new bitcoins created and introduced into the money supply? As we have already seen, because Bitcoin is a peer-to-peer network, there is no central authority charged with either creating currency units or verifying transactions. This network depends on users who provide their computing power to do the logging and reconciling of transactions. These users are called "miners"[13] because they are rewarded for their work with newly created bitcoins. Bitcoins are created, or "mined," as thousands of dispersed computers solve complex math problems that verify the transactions in the block chain. As one commentator has put it,

> The actual mining of Bitcoins is by a purely mathematical process. A useful analogy is with the search for prime numbers: it used to be fairly easy to find the small ones (Eratosthenes in Ancient Greece produced the first algorithm for finding them). But as they were found it got harder to find the larger ones. Nowadays researchers use advanced high-performance computers to find them and their achievements are noted by the mathematical community (for example, the University of Tennessee maintains a list of the highest 5,000).
>
> For Bitcoins the search is not actually for prime numbers but to find a sequence of data (called a "block") that produces a particular pattern when the Bitcoin "hash" algorithm is applied to the data. When a match occurs the miner obtains a bounty of Bitcoins (and also a fee if that block was used to certify a transaction). The size of the bounty reduces as Bitcoins

---

[11] "Markets," Bitcoincharts, accessed July 30, 2013, http://bitcoincharts.com/markets/.

[12] Christof Paar, Jan Pelzl, and Bart Preneel, "Introduction to Public-Key Cryptography," chapter 6 in *Understanding Cryptography: A Textbook for Students and Practitioners*, ed. Christof Paar and Jan Pelzl (New York: Springer, 2010). Sample available at http://wiki.crypto.rub.de/Buch/download/Understanding-Cryptography-Chapter6.pdf.

[13] Miners tend to be ordinary computer enthusiasts, but as mining becomes more difficult and expensive, the activity will likely become somewhat professionalized. For more information, see Alec Liu, "A Guide to Bitcoin Mining," *Motherboard*, March 22, 2013, http://motherboard.vice.com/blog/a-guide-to-bitcoin-mining-why-someone-bought-a-1500-bitcoin-miner-on-ebay-for-20600.

around the world are mined.

The difficulty of the search is also increased so that it becomes computationally more difficult to find a match. These two effects combine to reduce over time the rate at which Bitcoins are produced and mimic the production rate of a commodity like gold. At some point new Bitcoins will not be produced and the only incentive for miners will be transaction fees.[14]

So, the protocol was designed so that each miner contributes a computer's processing power toward maintaining the infrastructure needed to support and authenticate the currency network. Miners are awarded newly created bitcoins for contributing their processing power toward maintaining the network and verifying transactions in the block chain. And as more processing power is dedicated to mining, the protocol will increase the difficulty of the math problem, ensuring that bitcoins are always mined at a predictable and limited rate.

This process of mining bitcoins will not continue forever. Bitcoin was designed to mimic the extraction of gold or other precious metals from the earth—only a limited, known number of bitcoins can ever be mined. The arbitrary number chosen to be the cap is 21 million bitcoins. Miners are projected to painstakingly harvest the last "satoshi," or 0.00000001 of a bitcoin, in the year 2140. If the total mining power scales to a high enough level, the difficulty in mining bitcoins will have increased so much that procuring this last satoshi will be quite a challenging digital undertaking. Once the last satoshi has been mined, miners that contribute their processing power toward verifying transactions will be rewarded through transaction fees rather than mined bitcoins. This ensures that miners still have an incentive to keep the network running after the last bitcoin is mined.

Pseudonymity

A great deal of attention given to Bitcoin in the media centers on the anonymity that the digital currency is supposed to lend its users. This idea stems from a mistaken understanding of the currency, however.

Because online transactions to date have required a third-party intermediary, they have not been anonymous. PayPal, for example, will have a record of every time Alice has sent Bob money. And because Alice's and Bob's PayPal accounts are tied to their respective bank accounts, their identities are likely known. In contrast, if Alice gives Bob a $100 bill in cash, there is no intermediary and no record of the transaction. And if Alice and Bob don't know each other's identities, we can say the transaction is completely anonymous.

Bitcoin falls somewhere between these two extremes. On the one hand, bitcoins are like cash in that once Alice gives bitcoins to Bob, she no longer has them and Bob does, and there is no third-party intermediary between them that knows their respective identities. On the other hand, unlike cash, the fact that a transaction took place between two public keys, the time, the amount, and other information is recorded in the block chain. Indeed, every transaction that has ever occurred in the history of the bitcoin economy is publicly viewable in the block chain.[15]

While the public keys for all transactions—also known as "Bitcoin addresses"[16]—are

---

[14] Ken Tindell, "Geeks Love the Bitcoin Phenomenon Like They Loved the Internet in 1995," *Business Insider*, April 5, 2013, http://www.businessinsider.com/how-bitcoins-are-mined-and-used-2013-4.

[15] Note that this might be a boon to economic researchers.

[16] *Bitcoin wiki*, s.v. "Address," accessed July 30, 2013, https://en.bitcoin.it/wiki/Address.

recorded in the block chain, those public keys are not tied to anyone's identity. Yet if a person's identity were linked to a public key, one could look through the recorded transactions in the block chain and easily see all transactions associated with that key. So, while Bitcoin is very similar to cash in that parties can transact without disclosing their identities to a third party or to each other, it is unlike cash in that all the transactions to and from a particular Bitcoin address can be traced. In this way Bitcoin is not anonymous, but pseudonymous.

Tying a real-world identity to a pseudonymous Bitcoin address is not as difficult as some might imagine. For one thing, a person's identity (or at least identifying information, such as an IP address) is often recorded when the person makes a Bitcoin transaction at a website, or exchanges dollars for bitcoins at a bitcoin exchange. To increase the chances of remaining pseudonymous, one would have to employ anonymizing software like Tor, and take care never to transact with Bitcoin addresses that could be tied back to one's identity.

Finally, it is also possible to glean identities simply by looking at the block chain. One study found that behavior-based clustering techniques could reveal the identities of 40 percent of Bitcoin users in their simulated Bitcoin experiment.[17] An early analysis of the statistical properties of the Bitcoin transaction graph showed how a passive network analysis with the appropriate tools can divulge the financial activity and identities of Bitcoin users.[18] A later analysis of the statistical properties of the Bitcoin transaction graph garnered similar results with a larger dataset.[19] Another analysis of the Bitcoin transaction graph reiterated that observers using "entity merging"[20] can observe structural patterns in user behavior and emphasized that this is "one of the most important challenges to Bitcoin anonymity."[21] In spite of this, Bitcoin users do enjoy a much higher level of privacy than do users of traditional digital-transfer services, who must provide detailed personal information to the third-party financial intermediaries that facilitate the exchange.

Although Bitcoin is frequently referred to as an "anonymous" currency, in reality, it is very difficult to stay anonymous in the Bitcoin network. Pseudonyms tied to transactions recorded in the public ledger can be identified years after an exchange is made. Once Bitcoin intermediaries are fully compliant with the bank-secrecy regulations required of traditional financial intermediaries, anonymity will be even less guaranteed, because Bitcoin intermediaries will be required to collect personal data on their customers.

Benefits

The first question that many people have when they learn about Bitcoin is, Why would I want to use bitcoins when I can use dollars? Bitcoin is still a new and fluctuating currency that is not accepted by many merchants, so the uses for Bitcoin may seem mostly experimental. To better

---

[17] Elli Androulaki et al., "Evaluating User Privacy in Bitcoin," *IACR Cryptology ePrint Archive* 596 (2012), http://fc13.ifca.ai/proc/1-3.pdf.

[18] Fergal Reid and Martin Harrigan, "An Analysis of Anonymity in the Bitcoin System," in *Security and Privacy in Social Networks*, ed. Yaniv Altshuler et al. (New York: Springer, 2013), http://arxiv.org/pdf/1107.4524v2.pdf.

[19] Dorit Ron and Adi Shamir, "Quantitative Analysis of the Full Bitcoin Transaction Graph," *IACR Cryptology ePrint Archive* 584 (2012), http://eprint.iacr.org/2012/584.pdf.

[20] Entity merging is the process of observing two or more public keys used as an input to one transaction at the same time. In this way, even if a user has several different public keys, an observer can gradually link them together and remove the ostensible anonymity that multiple public keys is thought to provide.

[21] Micha Ober, Stefan Katzenbeisser, and Kay Hamacher, "Structure and Anonymity of the Bitcoin Transaction Graph," *Future Internet* 5, no. 2 (2013), http://www.mdpi.com/1999-5903/5/2/237.

understand why people might want to use Bitcoin, it helps to think of it, not necessarily as a replacement for traditional currencies, but rather as a new payments system.

Lower Transaction Costs

Because there is no third-party intermediary, Bitcoin transactions are substantially cheaper and quicker than traditional payment networks. And because transactions are cheaper, Bitcoin makes micropayments and other innovations possible. Additionally, Bitcoin holds much promise as a way to lower transaction costs for small businesses and global remittances, alleviate global poverty by improving access to capital, protect individuals against capital controls and censorship, ensure financial privacy for oppressed groups, and spur innovation (within and on top of the Bitcoin protocol). On the other hand, Bitcoin's decentralized nature also presents opportunities for crime. The challenge, then, is to develop processes that diminish the opportunities for criminality while maintaining the benefits that Bitcoin can provide.

First, Bitcoin is attractive to cost-conscious small businesses looking for ways to lower the transaction costs of doing business. Credit cards have greatly expanded the ease of transacting, but their use comes with considerable costs to merchants. Businesses that wish to offer the option of credit card payments to their customers must first pay for a merchant account with each credit card company. Depending on the terms of agreement with each credit card company, businesses must then pay a variety of authorization fees, transaction fees, statement fees, interchange fees, and customer-service fees, among other charges. These fees quickly add up and significantly increase the cost of doing business. However, if a merchant neglects to accept credit card payments to save on fees, he or she could lose a considerable amount of business from customers who enjoy the ease of credit cards.

Since Bitcoin facilitates direct transactions without a third party, it removes costly charges that accompany credit card transactions. The Founders Fund, the venture capital fund headed by Peter Thiel of PayPal and Facebook fame, recently invested $3 million in the payment-processing company BitPay because of the service's ability to lower the costs of doing online commerce across borders.[22] In fact, small businesses have already started to accept bitcoins as a way to avoid the costs of doing business with credit card companies.[23] Others have adopted the currency for its speed and efficiency in facilitating transactions.[24] Merchants labeled "high risk" by credit card companies have difficulty finding a payment processor willing to work with them, so they have turned to Bitcoin merchant services providers, like BitPay, as an affordable and convenient alternative to credit card services.[25] Bitcoin will likely continue to lower transaction costs for businesses that accept it as more people adopt the currency.

Accepting credit card payments also puts businesses on the hook for charge-back fraud.

---

[22] Tom Simonite, "Bitcoin Hits the Big Time, to the Regret of Some Early Boosters," *MIT Technology Review*, May 22, 2013, http://www.technologyreview.com/news/515061/bitcoin-hits-the-big-time-to-the-regret-of-some-early-boosters/.

[23] Gabrielle Karol, "Small Business Owners Say Bitcoins Better Than Credit Cards," *FOX Business, Small Business Center*, April 12, 2013, http://smallbusiness.foxbusiness.com/entrepreneurs/2013/04/12/small-business-owners-say-bitcoins-better-than-credit-cards/.

[24] Bailey Reutzel, "Why Some Merchants Accept Bitcoin Despite the Risks," *Payments Source*, May 21, 2013, http://www.paymentssource.com/news/why-some-merchants-accept-bitcoin-despite-the-risks-3014183-1.html.

[25] Bailey Reutzel, "Some Risky Merchants Turn to Bitcoin Processor; Others Go It Alone," *Payments Source*, November 8, 2013, http://www.paymentssource.com/news/some-risky-merchants-turn-to-bitcoin-processor-others-go-it-alone-3015974-1.html.

Merchants have long been plagued by fraudulent "charge-backs," or consumer-initiated payment reversals based on a false claim that a product has not been delivered.[26] Merchants therefore can lose the payment for the item and the item itself, and also have to pay a fee for the charge-back. As a nonreversible payment system, Bitcoin eliminates the "friendly fraud" wrought by the misuse of consumer charge-backs. This can be very important for small businesses. As Dan Lee, the manager of a small bodega in Brooklyn, puts it, "[With Bitcoin], there are lower fees, and you don't have to worry about charge-backs, which is beneficial for merchants. It's better than Visa or MasterCard."[27] This property is so valuable to the business that Lee's Greene Avenue Market offers a 10% discount to customers who pay in Bitcoin.

Consumers like charge-backs, however, because that system protects them from unscrupulous merchants or merchant errors. Consumers may also enjoy other benefits that merchant-account fees help fund. Indeed, many consumers and merchants will probably stick to traditional credit card services even if Bitcoin payments become available. Still, the expanded choices in payment options would benefit people of all preferences.

Those who want the protection and perks of using a credit card can continue to do so, even if they pay a little more. Those who are more price- or privacy-conscious can use bitcoins instead. Not having to pay merchant fees means that merchants who accept Bitcoin have the option to pass the savings on to consumers. That is the business model of the Bitcoin Store,[28] which sells thousands of consumer electronics at discounted prices and only accepts bitcoins. The same Samsung Galaxy Note tablet that sells on Amazon for $779 plus shipping[29] sells at the Bitcoin Store for a mere $480.[30] In this way, Bitcoin provides more low-cost options to bargain hunters and small businesses without detracting from the traditional credit card services that some consumers prefer.

As an inexpensive funds-transfer system, Bitcoin also holds promise for the future of low-cost remittances. In 2012, immigrants to developed countries sent at least $401 billion in remittances back to relatives living in developing countries.[31] The amount of remittances is projected to increase to $515 billion by 2015.[32] Most of these remittances are sent using traditional brick-and-mortar wire services such as Western Union and MoneyGram, which

---

[26] Emily Maltby, "Chargebacks Create Business Headaches," *Wall Street Journal*, February 10, 2011, http://online.wsj.com/article/SB10001424052748704698004576104554234202010.html. One such scam involves Alice sending Bob a PayPal payment for a laptop that Bob has listed on Craigslist. Alice comes by Bob's house, picks up the laptop, and soon thereafter initiates a "charge-back" (i.e., reverses the payment). PayPal generally requires proof of shipment before reversing a charge-back, so Bob is out of luck.

[27] Rob Wile, "A Brooklyn Bodega Owner Told Us Why All Merchants Should Start Accepting Bitcoin," *Business Insider*, November 11, 2013, http://www.businessinsider.com/brooklyn-bitcoin-bodega-2013-11.

[28] Vitalik Buterin, "Bitcoin Store Opens: All Your Electronics Cheaper with Bitcoins," *Bitcoin Magazine*, November 5, 2012, http://bitcoinmagazine.com/bitcoin-store-opens-all-your-electronics-cheaper-with-bitcoins/.

[29] Amazon listing for a Samsung Galaxy Note tablet, accessed May 29, 2013, http://amzn.com/B00BJXNGIK.

[30] Bitcoin store listing for a Samsung Galaxy Note tablet, accessed May 29, 2013, https://www.bitcoinstore.com/samsung-galaxy-note-gt-n8013-10-1-32-gb-tablet-wi-fi-1-40-ghz-deep-gray.html. Products on the Bitcoin store are priced in both bitcoins and US dollars. At the point of purchase, Bitpay, a Bitcoin payment processing company, determines the currency conversion rate and holds that price for 15 minutes. See the Bitcoin Store FAQ: https://www.bitcoinstore.com/faq.

[31] World Bank Payment Systems Development Group, *Remittance Prices Worldwide: An Analysis of Trends in the Average Total Cost of Migrant Remittance Services* (Washington, DC: World Bank, 2013), http://remittanceprices.worldbank.org/~/media/FPDKM/Remittances/Documents/RemittancePriceWorldwide-Analysis-Mar2013.pdf.

[32] Ibid.

charge steep fees for the service and can take several business days to transfer the funds.[33] In the first quarter of 2013, the global average fee for sending remittances was 9.05 percent.[34] In contrast, transaction fees on the Bitcoin network tend to be less than 0.0005 BTC,[35] or 1 percent of the transaction.[36] This entrepreneurial opportunity to improve money transfers has attracted investments from big-name venture capitalists.[37] Even MoneyGram and Western Union are contemplating whether to integrate Bitcoin into their business models.[38] Bitcoin allows for instantaneous, inexpensive remittances, and the reduction in the cost of global remittances for consumers could be considerable.

Potential to Combat Poverty and Oppression

Bitcoin also has the potential to improve the quality of life for the world's poorest. Improving access to basic financial services is a promising antipoverty technique.[39] According to one estimate, 64 percent of people living in developing countries lack access to these services, perhaps because it is too costly for traditional financial institutions to serve poor, rural areas.[40] Because of the impediments to developing traditional branch banking in poor areas, people in developing countries have turned to mobile banking services for their financial needs. The closed-system mobile payment service M-Pesa has been particularly successful in countries such as Kenya, Tanzania, and Afghanistan.[41] Entrepreneurs are already moving to this model; the Bitcoin wallet service Kipochi recently developed a product that allows M-Pesa users to exchange bitcoins.[42] Mobile banking services in developing countries can be further augmented by the adoption of Bitcoin.

Other Bitcoin business models seek to streamline Bitcoin use in developing economies. LocalBitcoins.com, a listing and escrow service for individual small Bitcoin traders, publicizes trader information in over 190 countries, including Bangladesh, Zimbabwe, the Democratic Republic of Congo, Pakistan, Venezuela, Romania, India, Libya, and other developing economies.[43] The Google- and YCombinator-backed service provider startup, Buttercoin, aims to spread Bitcoin use in the developing world by partnering with locally licensed exchange

---

[33] Jessica Silver-Greenberg, "New Rules for Money Transfers, but Few Limits," *New York Times*, June 1, 2012, http://www.nytimes.com/2012/06/02/business/new-rules-for-money-transfers-but-few-limits.html?pagewanted=all&_r=0.
[34] World Bank, *Remittance Prices*.
[35] *Bitcoin wiki*, s.v. "Transaction fees," accessed July 30, 2013, https://en.bitcoin.it/wiki/Transaction_fees.
[36] Andrew Paul, "Is Bitcoin the Next Generation of Online Payments?," *Yahoo! Small Business Advisor*, May 24, 2013, http://smallbusiness.yahoo.com/advisor/bitcoin-next-generation-online-payments-213922448--finance.html.
[37] Simonite, "Bitcoin Hits the Big Time."
[38] Andrew R. Johnson, "Money Transfers in Bitcoins? Western Union, MoneyGram Weigh the Option," *Wall Street Journal*, April 18, 2013, http://online.wsj.com/article/SB10001424127887324493704578431000719258048.html.
[39] Muhammad Yunus, *Banker to the Poor: Micro-lending and the Battle against World Poverty* (New York: Public Affairs, 2003).
[40] Oya Pinar Ardic, Maximilien Heimann, and Nataliya Mylenko, "Access to Financial Services and the Financial Inclusion Agenda around the World" (Policy Research Working Paper, World Bank Financial and Private Sector Development Consultative Group to Assist the Poor, 2011), https://openknowledge.worldbank.org/bitstream/handle/10986/3310/WPS5537.pdf.
[41] Jeff Fong, "How Bitcoin Could Help the World's Poorest People," *PolicyMic*, May 2013, http://www.policymic.com/articles/41561/bitcoin-price-2013-how-bitcoin-could-help-the-world-s-poorest-people.
[42] Emily Spaven, "Kipochi launches M-Pesa Integrated Bitcoin Wallet in Africa," *CoinDesk*, July 19, 2013, http://www.coindesk.com/kipochi-launches-m-pesa-integrated-bitcoin-wallet-in-africa/.
[43] "Bitcoin Statistics," LocalBitcoins.com, accessed November 12, 2013, https://localbitcoins.com/statistics.

businesses to trade bitcoins for local currencies. By providing Bitcoin services to already-licensed companies in countries all over the world, Buttercoin can penetrate local markets without sacrificing compliance.[44] The company plans to open services in India by the end of 2013 and extend operations to six different countries in the following six months.[45]

Charities in the United States also have looked to Bitcoin as a promising way to alleviate poverty. Bitcoin's ease and affordability in transferring funds makes it an attractive option to lower operation costs for cash-strapped charities. The Bitcoin100 charity campaign has contributed Bitcoin donations to a number of causes since 2011.[46] Sean's Outpost, a homeless outreach organization located in Pensacola, Florida, has been providing meals and toiletries to Pensacola's neediest solely with bitcoins.[47] The charity's founder, Jason King, plans to open a nine acre homeless sanctuary, fittingly titled "Satoshi Forest," paid for entirely with Bitcoin.[48] According to King, Bitcoin's low costs and ease of transfer make it an ideal currency for his charity. "Anyone being able to send money to us in the world instantaneously is very valuable, and we've gotten donations from over twenty-three different countries," he explains.[49] As an open-system payment service, Bitcoin can provide low-income people in developing and developed countries alike with inexpensive access to financial services on a global scale.

Bitcoin might also provide relief to people living in countries with strict capital controls. The total number of bitcoins that can be mined is capped and cannot be manipulated. There is no central authority that can reverse transactions or prevent the exchange of bitcoins between countries. Bitcoin therefore provides an escape hatch for people who desire an alternative to their country's devalued currencies or frozen capital markets. We have already seen examples of people turning to Bitcoin to evade the harmful effects of capital controls and central-bank mismanagement. Some Argentines, for instance, have adopted Bitcoin in response to the country's dual burdens of a 25 percent inflation rate and strict capital controls.[50] Consumer confidence, too, continues to plunge in Argentina.[51] Demand for bitcoins is so strong in Argentina that one popular bitcoin exchange is planning to open an Argentine office.[52] Argentine Bitcoin use continues to surge in the face of Argentina's capital mismanagement.[53] For example,

---

[44] Bailey Ruetzel, "Buttercoin Takes a Different Path to Handling Virtual Currency," *Payments Source*, September 9, 2013, http://www.paymentssource.com/news/buttercoin-takes-a-different-path-to-handling-virtual-currency-3015366-1.html.

[45] Kim-Mai Cutler, "YC-Backed Buttercoin Uses Bitcoin To Attack the $500B-A-Year Remittances Economy," *Techcrunch*, August 20, 2013, http://techcrunch.com/2013/08/20/buttercoin/.

[46] Vitalik Buterin, "Charity Focus: Sean's Outpost," *Bitcoin Magazine*, April 2013, http://bitcoinmagazine.com /sandbox/seansoutpost.pdf.

[47] Ibid.

[48] Vitalik Buterin, "Sean's Outpost Announces Satoshi Forest, Nine-Acre Sanctuary for the Homeless," *Bitcoin Magazine*, September 9, 2023, http://bitcoinmagazine.com/6939/seans-outpost-announces-satoshi-forest/.

[49] Meghan Lords, "Feeding and Housing the Homeless with Bitcoin," *Bitcoin Not Bombs*, August 16, 2013, http:// www.bitcoinnotbombs.com/feeding-and-housing-the-homeless-with-bitcoin/.

[50] Jon Matonis, "Bitcoin's Promise in Argentina," *Forbes*, April 27, 2013, http://www.forbes.com/sites/jonmatonis /2013/04/27/bitcoins-promise-in-argentina/.

[51] Roberto A. Ferdman, "Argentina's Unofficial Consumer Confidence Metric is Free-Falling Again," *Quartz*, October 23, 2013, http://qz.com/138498/argentinas-unofficial-consumer-confidence-metric-is-free-falling-again/.

[52] Camila Russo, "Bitcoin Dreams Endure to Savers Crushed by CPI: Argentina Credit," *Bloomberg*, April 16, 2013, http://www.bloomberg.com/news/2013-04-16/bitcoin-dreams-endure-to-savers-crushed-by-cpi-argentina-credit .html.

[53] Georgia Wells, "Bitcoin Downloads Surge in Argentina," *Wall Street Journal Money Beat*, July 17, 2013, http:// blogs.wsj.com/moneybeat/2013/07/17/bitcoin-downloads-surge-in-argentina/.

the Net Party, an Argentine political reform movement, was funded almost entirely with bitcoins. "There you can see the different: the speed of money," says founder Santiago Siri, "[Raising] the money would have taken eight weeks [using the official currency]; it took one hour with Bitcoin."[54]

Individuals in oppressive or emergency situations might also benefit from the financial privacy that Bitcoin can provide. There are many legitimate reasons why people seek privacy in their financial transactions. Spouses fleeing abusive partners need some way to discreetly spend money without being tracked. People seeking controversial health services desire financial privacy from family members, employers, and others who might judge their decisions. Recent experiences with despotic governments suggest that oppressed citizens would benefit greatly from the ability to make private transactions free from the grabbing hands of tyrants. Bitcoin provides some of the privacy that has traditionally been afforded through cash—with the added convenience of digital transfer.

Stimulus for Financial Innovation

One of the most promising applications of Bitcoin is as a platform for financial innovation. The Bitcoin protocol contains the digital blueprints for a number of useful financial and legal services that programmers can easily develop. Since bitcoins are, at their core, simply packets of data, they can be used to transfer, not only currencies, but also stocks, bets, and sensitive information.[55] Some of the features that are built into the Bitcoin protocol include micropayments, dispute mediations, assurance contracts, and smart property.[56] These features would allow for the easy development of Internet translation services, instantaneous processing for small transactions (like automatically metering Wi-Fi access), and Kickstarter-like crowdfunding services. Indeed, early initiatives have already materialized. The crowdfunding platform Pozible now allows project creators to amass microdonations in Bitcoin for minuscule transaction fees.[57] The payment platform Bitmonet provides internet content creators with a way to monetize their blog or portfolio with bitcoins.[58] Similarly, Beatcoin is a music delivery service powered through Bitcoin micropayments.[59] As the Bitcoin economy further matures, more of these innovative applications will continue to materialize.

Additionally, programmers can develop alternative protocols on top of the Bitcoin protocol in the same way that the Web and email are run on top of the Internet's TCP/IP protocol. One

---

[54] Ben Smith and Conz Preti, "Argentina's Net Party Is Ready for the Revolution," *Buzzfeed*, October 24, 2013, http://www.buzzfeed.com/bensmith/argentinas-net-party-is-ready-for-the-revolution.

[55] Jerry Brito, "The Top 3 Things I Learned at the Bitcoin Conference," *Reason*, May 20, 2013, http://reason.com /archives/2013/05/20/the-top-3-things-i-learned-at-the-bitcoi.

[56] Mike Hearn, "Bitcoin 2012 London: Mike Hearn," YouTube video, 28:19, posted by "QueuePolitely," September 27, 2012, http://www.youtube.com/watch?v=mD4L7xDNCmA. Smart property is a concept to control ownership of an item through agreements made in the Bitcoin block chain. Smart property allows people to exchange ownership of a good or service once a condition is met using cryptography. Although smart property is still theoretical, the basic mechanisms are built into the Bitcoin protocol. See *Bitcoin wiki*, s.v., "Smart Property," accessed July 30, 2013, https://en.bitcoin.it/wiki/Smart_Property.

[57] "Pozible Now Accepting Pledges in Bitcoin," *Pozible Blog*, October 2013, http://www.pozible.com/blog/article /index/129.

[58] John Biggs, "Bitmonet Monetizes Your Blog Through the Power of Bitcoin, " *Techcrunch*, August 30, 2013, http://considertechcrunch.com/2013/08/30/bitmonet-monetizes-your-blog-through-the-power-of-bitcoin/.

[59] Romain Dillet, "Beatcoin is a Music Jukebox Hack Powered By Bitcoin Micropayments," *Techcrunch*, October 27, 2013, http://techcrunch.com/2013/10/27/beatcoin-is-a-music-jukebox-hack-powered-by-bitcoin-micropayments/.

programmer has already proposed a new protocol layer to add on top of the Bitcoin protocol that can improve the network's stability and security.[60] Another programmer created a digital notary service to anonymously and securely store a "proof of existence" for private documents on top of the Bitcoin protocol.[61] Other programmers have adopted the Bitcoin model as a way to encrypt email communications.[62] Another group of developers has outlined an add-on protocol that will improve the privacy of the network.[63] Bitcoin is thus the foundation upon which other layers of functionality can be built. The Bitcoin project can be best thought of as a process of financial and communicative experimentation. Policymakers should take care that their directives do not quash the promising innovations developing within and on top of this fledgling protocol.

Challenges

Despite the benefits that it presents, Bitcoin has some downsides for potential users to consider. It has exhibited considerable price volatility throughout its existence. New users are at risk of improperly securing or even accidentally deleting their bitcoins if they are not cautious. Additionally, there are concerns about whether hacking could compromise the bitcoin economy.

Volatility

Bitcoin has weathered at least five significant price adjustments since 2011.[64] These adjustments resemble traditional speculative bubbles: overoptimistic media coverage of Bitcoin prompts waves of novice investors to pump up Bitcoin prices.[65] The exuberance reaches a tipping point, and the value eventually plummets. Newcomer investors eager to participate run the risk of overvaluing the currency and losing their money in a crash. Bitcoin's fluctuating value makes many observers skeptical of the currency's future.

Does this volatility foretell the end of Bitcoin? Some commentators believe so.[66] Others suggest that these fluctuations are stress-testing the currency and might eventually decrease in frequency as mechanisms develop to counteract volatility.[67] If bitcoins were only used as stores of value or units of account, the currency's volatility could indeed endanger its future. It does not make sense to manage business finances or keep savings in bitcoins if the market price swings wildly and unpredictably. When Bitcoin is used as a medium of exchange, however, volatility is

---

[60] J. R. Willett, "The Second Bitcoin Whitepaper" (white paper, 2013), https://sites.google.com/site/2ndbtcwpaper /2ndBitcoinWhitepaper.pdf.

[61] Jeremy Kirk, "Could the Bitcoin Network Be Used as an Ultrasecure Notary Service?," *ComputerWorld*, May 23, 2013, http://www.computerworld.com/s/article/9239513/Could_the_Bitcoin_network_be_used_as_an_ultrasecure _notary_service_.

[62] Jonathan Warren, "Bitmessage: A Peer-to-Peer Message Authentication and Delivery System" (white paper, November 27, 2012), https://bitmessage.org/bitmessage.pdf.

[63] Ian Miers et al., "Zerocoin: Anonymous Distributed E-Cash from Bitcoin" (working paper, the Johns Hopkins University Department of Computer Science, Baltimore, MD, 2013), http://spar.isi.jhu.edu/~mgreen /ZerocoinOakland.pdf.

[64] Timothy B. Lee, "An Illustrated History of Bitcoin Crashes," *Forbes*, April 11, 2013, http://www.forbes.com/sites /timothylee/2013/04/11/an-illustrated-history-of-bitcoin-crashes/.

[65] Felix Salmon, "The Bitcoin Bubble and the Future of Currency," *Medium*, April 3, 2013, https://medium.com /money-banking/2b5ef79482cb.

[66] Maureen Farrell, "Strategist Predicts End of Bitcoin," *CNNMoney*, May 14, 2013, http://money.cnn.com/2013/05 /14/investing/bremmer-bitcoin/index.html.

[67] Adam Gurri, "Bitcoins, Free Banking, and the Optional Clause," *Ümlaut*, May 6, 2013, http://theumlaut.com/2013 /05/06/bitcoins-free-banking-and-the-optional-clause/.

less of a problem.[68] Merchants can price their wares in terms of a traditional currency and accept the equivalent number of bitcoins. Customers who purchase bitcoins to make a one-time purchase don't care about what the exchange rate will look like tomorrow; they simply care that Bitcoin can lower transaction costs in the present. Bitcoin's usefulness as a medium of exchange might explain why the currency has grown more popular among merchants in spite of its price volatility.[69] It is also possible that the value of bitcoins will become less volatile as more people become familiar with the Bitcoin technology and develop realistic expectations about its future.

Security Breaches

As a digital currency, Bitcoin presents some specific security challenges.[70] If people are not careful, they can inadvertently delete or misplace their bitcoins. Once the digital file is lost, the money is lost, just as with paper cash. If people do not protect their private Bitcoin addresses, they can leave themselves open to theft. Bitcoin wallets can now be protected by encryption, but users must choose to activate the encryption. If a user does not encrypt his or her wallet, bitcoins could be stolen through malware.[71] Bitcoin exchanges, too, have at times struggled with security; hackers successfully stole 24,000 BTC ($250,000) from a bitcoin exchange called Bitfloor in 2012[72] and mounted a massive series of distributed denial-of-service (DDoS) attacks against the most popular bitcoin exchange, Mt.Gox, in 2013.[73] (Bitfloor eventually repaid the stolen funds to its customers, and Mt.Gox ultimately recovered from the DDoS attacks.) More recently, the wallet and mixing service inputs.io lost an equivalent of $1.2 million of their customers' bitcoins to a hacking attack.[74] Unscrupulous exchange stewards have similarly been a problem; in November of 2013, GBL, a Chinese Bitcoin exchange, abruptly closed its website and absconded with $4.1 million worth of their customers' bitcoins.[75] While the accountable operator of inputs.io will compensate his customers with a partial refund, GBL customers are not so lucky. Combined with the GBL operators' duplicity, Bitcoin's irreversibility eradicates the possibility of recourse. Of course, many of the security risks facing Bitcoin are similar to those facing traditional currencies. Dollar bills can be destroyed or lost, personal financial information can be stolen and used by criminals, and banks can be robbed or targeted by DDoS attacks. Bitcoin users should take care to learn about and prepare for security concerns just as they currently do

---

[68] Jerry Brito, "Why Bitcoin's Valuation Really Doesn't Matter," *Technology Liberation Front*, April 5, 2013, http://techliberation.com/2013/04/05/why-bitcoins-valuation-doesnt-really-matter/.

[69] Today, merchant service providers accept the risk presented by the volatility and nevertheless maintain low fees. It remains to be seen whether this model will be sustainable in the long run.

[70] Most of the security challenges concern wallet services and bitcoin exchanges. The protocol itself has proven to be considerably resilient to hacking and security risks. Renowned security researcher Dan Kaminsky tried, but failed, to hack the Bitcoin protocol in 2011. See Dan Kaminsky, "I Tried Hacking Bitcoin and I Failed," *Business Insider*, April 12, 2013, http://www.businessinsider.com/dan-kaminsky-highlights-flaws-bitcoin-2013-4.

[71] Stephen Doherty, "All Your Bitcoins Are Ours . . . ," *Symantec Blog*, June 16, 2011, http://www.symantec.com/connect/blogs/all-your-bitcoins-are-ours.

[72] Devin Coldewey, "$250,000 Worth of Bitcoins Stolen in Net Heist," *NBC News*, September 5, 2012, http://www.nbcnews.com/technology/250-000-worth-bitcoins-stolen-net-heist-980871.

[73] Meghan Kelly, "Fool Me Once: Bitcoin Exchange Mt.Gox Falls after Third DDoS Attack This Month," *VentureBeat*, April 21, 2013, http://venturebeat.com/2013/04/21/mt-gox-ddos/.

[74] Robert McMillan, "$1.2M Hack Shows Why You Should Never Store Bitcoins on the Internet," *Wired*, November 7, 2013, http://www.wired.com/wiredenterprise/2013/11/inputs/.

[75] Jim Edwards, "A Bitcoin Exchange Holding $4.1 Million for 1,000 Customers Has Simply Vanished," *Business Insider*, November 12, 2013.

for other financial activities.

Criminal Uses

There are also reasons for policymakers to be apprehensive about some of Bitcoin's exaptations. Because Bitcoin is pseudonymous, policymakers and journalists have questioned whether criminals can use it to launder money and accept payment for illicit goods and services. Indeed, like cash, it can be used for ill as well as for good.

For one example, we can look at the shuttered Deep Web[76] black-market site known as "Silk Road." While in operation from February 2011 to October 2013, Silk Road took advantage of the anonymizing network Tor and the pseudonymous nature of Bitcoin to make available a vast digital marketplace where one could mail-order drugs and other licit and illicit wares. Although Silk Road administrators did not allow the exchange of any goods that resulted from fraud or harm, like stolen credit card information or photographs of child exploitation, it did allow merchants to sell illegal products like forged identity documents and illicit drugs. The pseudonymous nature of Bitcoin allowed buyers to purchase illegal goods online in the same way that cash has been traditionally used to facilitate illicit purchases in person. One study estimated the total monthly Silk Road transactions amounted to approximately $1.2 million.[77] But the Bitcoin market amassed $770 million in transactions during June 2013; Silk Road sales constituted a small drop in the total bitcoin economy bucket.[78]

Bitcoin's association with Silk Road has tarnished its reputation. Following the publication of an article on Silk Road in 2011,[79] senators Charles Schumer and Joe Manchin sent a letter to Attorney General Eric Holder and the Drug Enforcement Administration's administrator Michele Leonhart calling for a crackdown on Silk Road, the anonymizing software Tor, and Bitcoin.[80] Their concerns were quickly addressed. Following a two year investigation into the Deep Web market, the FBI shut down the Silk Road website on October 2, 2013 and arrested Ross Ulbricht, the man alleged to be its infamous operator known only as the "Dread Pirate Roberts."[81] The FBI confiscated all bitcoins associated with Silk Road, totaling an unprecedented seizure of 26,000 BTC, worth $3.6 million at the time of the transfer.[82] Many of the largest merchants on Silk Road, too, have been indicted since Silk Road's closure.[83] Still, the end of Silk Road has not eliminated the problem of illicit trade. Other Deep Web black markets, like Black Market

---

[76] *Wikipedia*, s.v. "Deep Web," accessed July 30, 2013, http://en.wikipedia.org/wiki/Deep_Web.

[77] Nicolas Christin, "Traveling the Silk Road: A Measurement Analysis of a Large Anonymous Online Marketplace," *Carnegie Mellon CyLab Technical Reports: CMU-CyLab-12-018*, July 30, 2012 (updated November 28, 2012), http://www.cylab.cmu.edu/files/pdfs/tech_reports/CMUCyLab12018.pdf.

[78] Jerry Brito, "*National Review* Gets Bitcoin Very Wrong," *Technology Liberation Front*, June 20, 2013, http://techliberation.com/2013/06/20/national-review-gets-bitcoin-very-wrong/.

[79] Adrian Chen, "The Underground Website Where You Can Buy Any Drug Imaginable," *Gizmodo*, June 1, 2011, http://gawker.com/5805928/the-underground-website-where-you-can-buy-any-drug-imaginable.

[80] Brett Wolf, "Senators Seek Crackdown on 'Bitcoin' Currency," *Reuters*, June 8, 2011, http://www.reuters.com/article/2011/06/08/us-financial-bitcoins-idUSTRE7573T320110608.

[81] Emily Flitter, "FBI Shuts Alleged online Drug Marketplace, Silk Road," *Reuters*, October 2, 2013, http://www.reuters.com/article/2013/10/02/us-crime-silkroad-raid-idUSBRE9910TR20131002.

[82] James Ball, Charles Arthur, and Adam Gabbatt, "FBI Claims Largest Bitcoin Seizure After Arrest of Alleged Silk Road Founder," *The Guardian*, October 2, 2013, http://www.theguardian.com/technology/2013/oct/02/alleged-silk-road-website-founder-arrested-bitcoin.

[83] Brian Krebs, "Feds Arrest Alleged Top Silk Road Drug Dealer," *Krebs on Security*, October 7, 2013, http://krebsonsecurity.com/2013/10/feds-arrest-alleged-top-silk-road-drug-seller/.

Reloaded,[84] Sheep Marketplace,[85] and the relaunched Silk Road 2.0,[86] present new challenges for law enforcement.

Another concern is that Bitcoin can be used to launder money for financing terrorism and trafficking in illegal goods. Although these worries are currently more theoretical than evidential, Bitcoin could indeed be an option for those who wish to discreetly move ill-gotten money. Concerns about Bitcoin's potential to facilitate money laundering were stoked after Liberty Reserve, a private, centralized digital-currency service based in Costa Rica, was shut down by authorities on charges of money laundering.[87]

While Liberty Reserve and Bitcoin appear similar because they both provide digital currencies, there are important differences between the two. Liberty Reserve was a centralized currency service created and owned by a private company, allegedly for the express purpose of facilitating money laundering. Bitcoin is not. The transactions within the Liberty Reserve economy were not transparent. Indeed, Liberty Reserve promised its customers anonymity. Bitcoin, on the other hand, is a decentralized open currency that provides a public record of all transactions. Money launderers may attempt to protect their Bitcoin addresses and identities, but their transaction records will always be public and accessible at any time by law enforcement. Laundering money through Bitcoin, then, can be seen as a much riskier undertaking than using a centralized system like Liberty Reserve. Additionally, several bitcoin exchanges have taken steps to comply with anti–money laundering record-keeping and reporting requirements.[88] The combination of a public ledger system and the cooperation of bitcoin exchanges in collecting information on their customers will likely make Bitcoin less attractive to launderers relative to private anonymous virtual currencies.

It is also important to note that many of the potential downsides of Bitcoin are the same as those facing traditional cash. Cash has historically been the vehicle of choice for drug traffickers and money launderers, but policymakers would never seriously consider banning cash. As regulators begin to contemplate Bitcoin, they should be wary of the perils of overregulation. In the worst-case scenario, regulators could prevent legitimate businesses from benefitting from the Bitcoin network without preventing money launderers and drug traffickers from using bitcoins. If bitcoin exchanges are overburdened by regulation and shut down, for instance, money launderers and drug traffickers could still put money into the network by paying a person in cash to transfer his or her bitcoins into their virtual wallets. In this scenario, beneficial transactions are prevented by overregulation while the targeted activities are still able to occur. The challenge for policymakers and regulators is how to develop a system of oversight that assuages their twin concerns about money laundering and illicit purchases without smothering the benefits that

---

[84] Ryan Mac, "False Alarm: Silk Road Competitor Black Market Reloaded Staying Online," *Forbes*, October 18, 2013, http://www.forbes.com/sites/ryanmac/2013/10/18/false-alarm-silk-road-competitor-black-market-reloaded-staying-online/.

[85] Leonid Bershidsky, "Goodbye Silk Road, Hello Sheep Marketplace," *Bloomberg*, October 4, 2013, http://www.bloomberg.com/news/2013-10-04/goodbye-silk-road-hello-sheep-marketplace.html.

[86] Andy Greenberg, "'Silk Road 2.0' Launches, Promising A Resurrected Black Market for the Dark Web," *Forbes*, November 6, 2013, http://www.forbes.com/sites/andygreenberg/2013/11/06/silk-road-2-0-launches-promising-a-resurrected-black-market-for-the-dark-web/.

[87] "Liberty Reserve Digital Money Service Forced Offline," *BBC News—Technology*, May 27, 2013, http://www.bbc.co.uk/news/technology-22680297.

[88] Jeffrey Sparshott, "Bitcoin Exchange Makes Apparent Move to Play by U.S. Money-Laundering Rules," *Wall Street Journal*, June 28, 2013, http://online.wsj.com/article/SB10001424127887323873904578574000957464468.html.

Bitcoin is poised to provide to legitimate users in their everyday lives.

REGULATION

Current law and regulation does not envision a technology like Bitcoin, so it exists in something of a legal gray area. This is largely the case because Bitcoin does not exactly fit existing statutory definitions of currency or other financial instruments or institutions, making it difficult to know which laws apply and how.

This situation is reminiscent of regulatory uncertainty surrounding other new technologies, such as Voice over Internet Protocol (VoIP).[89] When VoIP first emerged, the Communications Act and Federal Communications Commission (FCC) regulations only contemplated voice communications over the traditional public switched telephone network. Like Bitcoin, VoIP competed with a highly regulated legacy network, was less expensive, and was often peer-to-peer. To this day Congress and the FCC continue to grapple with VoIP policy questions, including which public-interest obligations should be required of VoIP providers and whether VoIP providers must comply with law-enforcement wiretap requests.

Luckily, however, Congress and the FCC have charted a path for VoIP that has clarified much of the regulatory ambiguity without saddling the new technology with the legacy regulatory burden intended for monopoly telephone service. As a result, VoIP has flourished as a technology, has introduced competition to a previously stagnant market, and has lowered costs and improved access for consumers. Policymakers should seek to achieve the same with Bitcoin.

Bitcoin has the properties of an electronic payments system, a currency, and a commodity, among other things. As a result, it will likely receive scrutiny from several regulators. Below is an outline of some of the questions confronting these agencies as they prepare to regulate Bitcoin.

Is Private Currency Legal?

One of the most common initial questions about Bitcoin is whether the online currency is legal, given the federal government's monopoly on issuing legal tender. The answer seems to be yes. The Constitution only prohibits the states from coining money.[90] Privately issued currencies are not forbidden, and in fact many local currencies are in circulation.[91] To promote local economies, businesspeople and lawmakers have developed several alternative currencies in recent years, such as the Cascadia Hour Exchange in Portland and Life Dollars in Bellingham, Washington.[92]

What private parties may not do is issue currency that resembles US money.[93] One notorious case is that of Bernard von NotHaus, who was convicted in 2011 after printing and distributing a gold-backed currency called the "Liberty Dollar." His crime was not that he issued an alternative currency, but that it was similar in appearance to the US dollar and that von NotHaus attempted

---

[89] Sam Rozenfeld, "FCC'S VoIP Regulation Dilemma," *Telephony Your Way*, April 30, 2011, http://www.telephonyyourway.com/2011/04/30/fccs-voip-regulation-dilemma/.

[90] U.S. Const. art I § 10.

[91] Reuben Grinberg, "Bitcoin: An Innovative Alternative Digital Currency," *Hastings Science & Technology Law Journal* 4 (2011): 159–208.

[92] Blake Ellis, "Local Currencies: 'In the U.S. We Don't Trust,'" *CNN Money*, January 27, 2012, http://money.cnn.com/2012/01/17/pf/local_currency/index.htm.

[93] 18 U.S.C. §§ 485 and 486.

to spend his currency into circulation as dollars and encouraged others to do so as well.[94] In contrast, Bitcoin is in no danger of being confused with US currency.

Money-Transmission Laws

A business that transmits funds from one person to another is a money transmitter and in 48 states and the District of Columbia must obtain a license to operate.[95] Money transmitters are also subject to the Bank Secrecy Act (BSA) as implemented by regulations from FinCEN. Additionally, the USA PATRIOT Act made it a criminal offense to operate an unlicensed money-transmission business.[96]

The purpose of state licensing of money transmission has traditionally been consumer protection.[97] Because money transmitters (such as money-order issuers) are typically not FDIC-insured banks, consumers can be left holding the bag if a money transmitter does not forward the funds to the intended recipient. Licensing attempts to minimize this risk. Money-transmitter licensing in the States became widespread after the widely publicized defaults of several money-order companies in the 1980s.[98]

The BSA, on the other hand, is intended to prevent or detect money laundering and terrorist financing.[99] It requires money transmitters and other financial institutions to register with FinCEN, implement anti-money-laundering programs, keep records of their customers, and report suspicious transactions and other data.

Because it's not a company or legal entity, but instead a global peer-to-peer network, Bitcoin itself can't be said to be a money transmitter. The question then is, Do any of the actors in the Bitcoin ecosystem fit the statutory definitions of "money transmitter" that would subject them to state and federal regulation?

In March 2013, FinCEN issued guidance on the application of the BSA to virtual currencies, which include Bitcoin. The guidance defines three categories of persons potentially subject to its regulations as money transmitters:

> A *user* is a person that obtains virtual currency to purchase goods or services. An *exchanger* is a person engaged as a business in the exchange of virtual currency for real currency, funds, or other virtual currency. An *administrator* is a person engaged as a business in issuing (putting into circulation) a virtual currency, and who has the authority to redeem (to withdraw from circulation) such virtual currency.[100]

We can apply each of these definitions to persons in the Bitcoin ecosystem. The clearest

---

[94] Grinberg, "Bitcoin," 193n158.
[95] *Hearing on the Regulation of Non-bank Money Transmitter—Money Services Businesses*, 112th Congress (2012) (statement of Ezra C. Levine), testimony before the Subcommittee on Financial Institutions and Consumer Credit of the House Committee on Financial Services, http://financialservices.house.gov/uploadedfiles/hhrg-112-ba15-wstate-elevine-20120621.pdf.
[96] 18 U.S.C. § 1960.
[97] Aaron Greenspan, *Held Hostage: How the Banking Sector Has Distorted Financial Regulation and Destroyed Technological Progress* (Palo Alto, CA: Think Computer Corporation, 2011), http://www.thinkcomputer.com/corporate/whitepapers/heldhostage.pdf.
[98] Ibid., 3.
[99] 31 U.S.C. § 5311.
[100] FinCEN, *Application of FinCEN's Regulations*.

definition is that of an *exchanger*. If one is in the business of exchanging dollars for bitcoins or vice versa, then we can conclude that one is a money transmitter under this guidance and must register with FinCEN and comply with the relevant record-keeping and reporting requirements. Also, because states often look to FinCEN's determinations about which types of entities are or are not money transmitters, an exchanger likely must obtain state money-transmitter licenses as well.

Less straightforward are the obligations of mere "users" of Bitcoin. The guidance states that if one obtains bitcoins "to purchase real or virtual goods or services," then one is not a money transmitter and not subject to FinCEN's regulations. It does not explain, however, how the law applies if one obtains bitcoins *not* to purchase goods or services. Some other reasons why one might obtain bitcoins include (1) speculation that the price of bitcoins will go up, (2) simply because one trusts a virtual currency's stability more than that of a particular "real currency" (think of Argentina or Zimbabwe), or (3) because one wants to make a remittance to a family member overseas. In none of these cases would Bitcoin users be assured that they are exempted from FinCEN's registration, record-keeping, and reporting requirements. This creates an uncertain regulatory environment that might unduly dampen use of Bitcoin.

Most confusing is how the guidance applies to Bitcoin miners, who create new bitcoins by lending their computing power to the Bitcoin network. The third class of persons that it defines is "administrators," but the definition only applies to centralized virtual currencies in which a central authority creates the currency. For example, Amazon.com is clearly the administrator of its new "Amazon Coins" virtual currency.[101] The guidance, therefore, has a section addressing decentralized virtual currencies such as Bitcoin. According to that section, a miner who mines bitcoins and then uses them "to purchase real or virtual goods and services" is considered a user not subject to the regulations.[102] But if the miner sells the mined bitcoins "to another person for real currency or its equivalent" then the miner qualifies as a money transmitter subject to regulation.[103]

It is not clear how such regulation of miners as money transmitters would further either consumer protection or anti-money-laundering interests. Miners are not transmitting bitcoins from one party to another; they are creating new bitcoins from thin air. If miners sell the bitcoins they mine, there are only two parties to the transaction. As a result, there is neither a consumer to protect nor a potential criminal seeking to convert "dirty money" into clean money.

Finally, the guidance notes that FinCEN regulations define currency as the currency of a state, and so the guidance also refers to this definition as "real currency."[104] It then develops a new concept that it calls "virtual currency" on which all the guidance is predicated.[105] The guidance defines virtual currency as "a medium of exchange that operates like a currency in some environments, but does not have all the attributes of real currency."[106] It goes on to introduce another concept by stating that there are different kinds of "virtual currency" and that the present guidance only extends to "convertible virtual currency," which it defines as one that

---

[101] Ingrid Lunden, "Amazon Now Offers Amazon Coins Virtual Currency on Kindle Fire, Gives $5 in Free Coins to All Users," *TechCrunch*, May 13, 2013, http://techcrunch.com/2013/05/13/amazon-launches-amazon-coins-virtual-currency-on-kindle-fire-gives-5-in-free-coins-to-all-users/.

[102] Ibid.

[103] Ibid.

[104] FinCEN, *Application of FinCEN's Regulations.*

[105] Ibid.

[106] Ibid.

"either has an equivalent value in real currency, or acts as a substitute for real currency."[107] While the definition of currency (aka "real currency") was adopted through rulemaking, the other new and substantive concepts of "virtual currency" and "convertible virtual currency" exist only in the guidance. As a result, the guidance may be seen as encompassing new law and not merely interpretations of existing law or regulations, thus necessitating a rulemaking under the Administrative Procedure Act.

CFTC Regulation

By their nature, bitcoins can be conceived of either as a commodity or as a currency. Indeed, economist George Selgin has called Bitcoin "synthetic-commodity money."[108] This has attracted the attention of the Commodity Futures Trading Commission (CFTC), which has authority to regulate commodity futures and the markets in which they trade, as well as to regulate some foreign-exchange instruments.[109]

Bart Chilton, one of five CFTC commissioners, recently told the *Financial Times* that Bitcoin "is for sure something we need to explore."[110] Other sources confirmed that the CFTC is "seriously" looking at the virtual currency.[111] To the extent it chooses to regulate bitcoin transactions, one obvious question is whether CFTC will do so under its commodity futures or foreign-exchange authority.

While the Commodity Exchange Act defines "foreign-exchange forwards" and "foreign-exchange swaps," it does not define "foreign exchange" or "foreign currency," presumably because Congress considered the meaning of those terms obvious. Therefore, if the CFTC moves to apply its foreign-exchange regulations to Bitcoin transactions, it will have to make the determination that bitcoins are considered "foreign currency." While conceivable, such a determination would be at odds with the common understanding of foreign currency, as the money coined by foreign governments.

To illustrate this, we can look at the 2009 Dodd-Frank Wall Street Reform and Consumer Protection Act, which expands the CFTC's authority to regulate foreign exchange. Title 10 of the act also establishes the Consumer Financial Protection Bureau (CFPB), and for purposes of that title defines "foreign exchange" as "the exchange, for compensation, of currency of the United States or of a foreign government for currency of another government."[112] This definition gives a hint of what Congress's conception of "foreign exchange" is, and bitcoin exchange would clearly fall outside it, because bitcoins are not the currency of any government.

The connection between foreign currency and government issuance is commonplace. For example, the Treasury Department's definition of currency (adopted through rulemaking, as noted earlier) is

> the coin and paper money of the United States or of any other country that is designated as legal tender and that circulates and is customarily used and accepted as a medium of exchange in the country of issuance. Currency includes US silver certificates, US notes and

---

[107] Ibid.
[108] George Selgin, "Synthetic Commodity Money" (working paper, Department of Economics, University of Georgia, Athens, 2013), http://papers.ssrn.com/sol3/papers.cfm?abstract_id=2000118.
[109] 7 U.S.C. §§ 2(C) and 2(E).
[110] Alloway, Meyer, and Foley, "US Regulators Eye Bitcoin."
[111] Ibid.
[112] Dodd-Frank Wall Street Reform and Consumer Protection Act § 1002 (16); 12 U.S.C. § 5481 (16) (2012).

Federal Reserve notes. Currency also includes official foreign bank notes that are customarily used and accepted as a medium of exchange in a foreign country.[113]

This comports with the Uniform Commercial Code's definition of "money," which is "a medium of exchange authorized or adopted by a domestic or foreign government [including] a monetary unit of account established by an intergovernmental organization or by agreement between two or more nations."[114]

In contrast, the CFTC would have no problem treating bitcoins as commodities. The Commodity Exchange Act defines commodities as all "goods and articles . . . and all services, rights, and interests . . . in which contracts for future delivery are presently or in the future dealt in," except onions and motion-picture box-office receipts.[115] Therefore, bitcoins could certainly qualify as a commodity because they are articles that can be traded and made subject to futures contracts. That said, it is interesting to note that bitcoins are unlike traditional commodities such as gold, corn, or oil, which are tangible and have intrinsically valuable uses. It is also important to note that the CFTC's authority is over, not commodities themselves, but commodity futures. An exchange of bitcoins for dollars or other national currency, however, typically occurs instantaneously, and not as part of a futures contract. Therefore, CFTC regulation of bitcoins *as commodities* may be limited. To the extent bitcoin futures markets develop, however, they will certainly be subject to CFTC supervision.[116]

Electronic Fund Transfer Regulation

The final possible vector for regulation of Bitcoin under existing law that we will consider is regulation under the Electronic Fund Transfer Act (EFTA)[117] and its application through the Federal Reserve's Regulation E.[118] The purpose of the EFTA is to establish the respective rights and responsibilities of consumers and financial institutions in electronic fund transfers.[119] Like the other laws and regulations we have seen, the EFTA does not seem to contemplate a decentralized virtual currency like Bitcoin.

The act defines electronic fund transfers as "any transfer of funds, other than a transaction originated by check, draft, or similar paper instrument, which is initiated through an electronic terminal, telephonic instrument, or computer or magnetic tape so as to order, instruct, or authorize a financial institution to debit or credit an account."[120] It further defines "financial institution" as "a State or National bank, a State or Federal savings and loan association, a mutual savings bank, a State or Federal credit union, or any other person who, directly or indirectly, holds an account belonging to a consumer."[121] These definitions, and the regulations they undergird, assume that electronic fund transfers will necessarily involve "financial

---

[113] 31 C.F.R. § 1010.100(m).
[114] Unif. Commercial Code §§ 1–201.
[115] 7 U.S.C. § 1a (9).
[116] There are, however, emerging Bitcoin futures markets. See Cyrus Farivar, "'Taming the Bubble': Investors Bet on Bitcoin via Derivatives Markets," *Ars Technica*, April 11, 2013, http://arstechnica.com/business/2013/04/taming-the-bubble-investors-bet-on-bitcoin-via-derivatives-markets/.
[117] 15 U.S.C. §§ 1601–1692 (2013).
[118] 12 C.F.R. §§ 205.1–205.20.
[119] 15 U.S.C. § 1693(b).
[120] 15 U.S.C. § 1693a (7).
[121] 15 U.S.C. § 1693a (9).

institutions" and "accounts." Bitcoin, however, runs counter to that notion.

The Bitcoin system itself does not qualify as a "financial institution" because, as noted earlier, it is not a company or legal entity but instead a global peer-to-peer network. As a result, a Bitcoin address with which bitcoins are associated on the network cannot be said to be an account of a financial institution. Furthermore, as noted above in the technical discussion of how bitcoins are transferred between addresses, in the Bitcoin system there is no "financial institution" or other third party of any kind that "debit[s] or credit[s] an account." Electronic fund transfers between addresses are carried out by users alone, who sign a transaction with the private key associated with a Bitcoin address under their control. The Bitcoin network merely confirms that the transaction is legitimate.

While many users keep the "wallet files"[122] containing their private keys on their own computers or other devices,[123] some delegate securing their keys to online wallet services.[124] Such third-party wallet services often also provide greater ease-of-use than desktop Bitcoin software. Users typically create an "account" on such a wallet service, and their Bitcoin addresses are associated with those accounts. It is conceivable that such online services could fit the definition of "financial institution" under the EFTA, and thus be subject to the regulation. An argument could be made, however, that these services are not engaged in electronic fund transfers because they do not initiate transfers.[125] Transfers are made by the users directly and are verified by the Bitcoin network; online wallet services merely provide the software and storage that allows users to interact with the Bitcoin network.

Finally, new rules from the Consumer Financial Protection Bureau (CFPB) amending Regulation E target remittance-transfer providers. The regulations require remittance providers to disclose exchange rates and fees associated with international transfers, and to investigate and remediate processing errors.[126] They also require that consumers be afforded 30 minutes or more to cancel a transfer.[127] This requirement can be seen as incompatible with the Bitcoin protocol, because all bitcoin transactions are irreversible. One way to comply with this regulation might be to delay the execution of transactions. The real problem, though, is that this requirement is fundamentally at odds with the purpose of the technology.

Policy Recommendations

As we have seen, Bitcoin does not easily fit into existing regulatory boxes. That is often the hallmark of a disruptive technology. Indeed Bitcoin is a revolutionary technical achievement that heralds amazing potential benefits to human welfare. However, like any technology that can be used for good, it can also be used for ill. The challenge for policymakers will be to foster Bitcoin's beneficial uses while minimizing its negative consequences. We conclude with some recommendations to help policymakers meet this challenge.

---

[122] *Bitcoin wiki*, s.v. "Wallet," accessed July 30, 2013, https://en.bitcoin.it/wiki/Wallet.

[123] Matthew Sparks, "Winklevoss Twins Back Bitcoin as Bubble Bursts," *Telegraph*, April 12, 2013, http://www.telegraph.co.uk/technology/news/9989610/Winklevoss-twins-back-bitcoin-as-bubble-bursts.html.

[124] *Bitcoin wiki*, "EWallet," accessed July 30, 2013, https://en.bitcoin.it/wiki/EWallet.

[125] Nikolei M. Kaplanov, "Nerdy Money: Bitcoin, the Private Digital Currency, and the Case against Its Regulation," *Loyola Consumer Law Review* 25, no. 1 (2012).

[126] Consumer Financial Protection Bureau, "Summary of the Final Remittance Transfer Rule (Amendment to Regulation E)" (Washington, DC: Consumer Financial Protection Bureau, 2013), http://files.consumerfinance.gov/f/201305_cfpb_remittance-transfer-rule_summary.pdf.

[127] Ibid.

Don't Restrict Bitcoin

Because Bitcoin is essentially online cash, some who trade in drugs and other illicit goods online have found it to be an ideal medium of exchange.[128] Confronted with this fact, the initial impulse of some policymakers will be to call for restrictions on the technology.[129] There are many good reasons, however, to resist such an impulse.

First, as a technology, Bitcoin is neither good nor bad; it is neutral. Paper dollar bills, like bitcoins, can be used in illicit transactions, yet we do not consider outlawing paper bills. We only prohibit their *illicit use*. Furthermore, there is only anecdotal evidence about the extent to which bitcoins are utilized in criminal transactions. It would be wise to put the criminal use of the technology in perspective alongside its legitimate uses. As the bitcoin economy grows, legitimate uses of bitcoins will likely dwarf criminal transactions,[130] just as we see with paper dollar bills.

Second, any attempt to restrict Bitcoin technology will only harm legitimate uses while leaving illicit uses largely unaffected. Because it is a decentralized global network, Bitcoin is virtually impossible to shut down. There is no Bitcoin company or other entity that can be targeted. Instead, Bitcoin and its ledger exist only in the distributed peer-to-peer network created by its users. As with the peer-to-peer file-sharing service BitTorrent, taking down any of the individual computers that make up the peer-to-peer system would have little effect on the rest of the network. Therefore, making the use of Bitcoin illegal would not undermine the network; it would only serve to ensure that law-abiding users are denied access to the technology. As a result, society would forgo enjoying the many potential benefits of Bitcoin without seeing any drop in criminal use.

Third, if Bitcoin were prohibited, the government would forego the opportunity to regulate intermediaries in the bitcoin economy, such as exchangers and money transmitters. The governmental interests in detecting and preventing money laundering and terrorist financing would be better advanced, not by prohibiting the technology, but by requiring intermediaries to keep records and report suspicious activities, just as traditional financial institutions do. Again, restricting the use of Bitcoin will only ensure that criminals alone will use the technology. Any illicit intermediaries that emerge, such as exchanges and payment processors, will be unregulated.

Finally, even if the United States prohibited the use of Bitcoin, it is likely that many other countries would not, recognizing the technology's many potential benefits. The Finnish central bank, for example, has stated that the digital currency is not illegal,[131] and as a result many Finnish businesses have begun to accept bitcoins.[132] By prohibiting Bitcoin use, the United

---

[128] Andy Greenberg, "Founder of Drug Site Silk Road Says Bitcoin Booms and Busts Won't Kill His Black Market," *Forbes*, April 16, 2013, http://www.forbes.com/sites/andygreenberg/2013/04/16/founder-of-drug-site-silk-road-says-bitcoin-booms-and-busts-wont-kill-his-black-market/.

[129] Charles Schumer and Joe Manchin, Letter to Attorney General Eric Holder and Drug Enforcement Administration Administrator Michele Leonhart, June 6, 2011. Available at http://www.manchin.senate.gov/public/index.cfm/press-releases?ID=284ae54a-acf1-4258-be1c-7acee1f7e8b3.

[130] Jan Jahosky, "BitPay Eclipses Silk Road in Bitcoin Sales with Explosive $5.2M March," *BitPay Blog*, April 2, 2013, http://blog.bitpay.com/2013/04/bitpay-eclipses-silk-road-in-bitcoin.html.

[131] Matt Clinch, "Bitcoin Utopia? Interest Is Sky High in This Euro Nation," *CNBC*, April 4, 2013, http://www.cnbc.com/id/100618694.

[132] Jan Jahosky, "BitPay Exceeds 1,000 Merchants Accepting Bitcoin," *BitPay Blog*, September 11, 2012, http://blog.bitpay.com/2012/09/bitpay-exceeds-1000-merchants-accepting.html.

States could put itself at an international competitive disadvantage in the development and use of what may be the next-generation payments system.

Normalize Regulation and Encourage Further Development

Rather than overreact to illicit uses of Bitcoin, policymakers would be wise to take a calm and careful approach to the challenges posed by the new technology. Doing so would allow law enforcement to pursue its interests in detecting and preventing money laundering and terrorist financing while ensuring that society does not forgo Bitcoin's many benefits. Luckily, regulators to date have taken such a cautious approach by slowly integrating Bitcoin into the existing financial regulatory framework. Policymakers can take a few basic steps to maintain the right balance.

In the short term, FinCEN should clarify its recent guidance, especially as it relates to miners and users who do not obtain bitcoins to purchase goods or services, but instead do so for other legal and legitimate purposes. It should do this by welcoming public participation of the Bitcoin community of developers, miners, businesses, and users in formal public notice and comment proceedings. While FinCEN's mission is to safeguard the financial system from illicit use, it also has an obligation not to unduly hinder its technological development. Working with Bitcoin's legitimate users, there is no doubt FinCEN can achieve its goals while minimizing regulatory uncertainty.

In the long term, policymakers should better define Bitcoin's broader regulatory status. As we have seen, the digital currency does not comfortably fit any existing classification or legal definition. It is not a foreign currency, nor a traditional commodity, nor is it simply a payments network. Consequently, applying existing rules to Bitcoin could unduly impede Bitcoin's legitimate development without any attendant gains to law enforcement or consumer welfare. As a result, policymakers may want to consider developing a new category that takes into account the technology's unique nature. They should also carefully consider what regulation, if any, bitcoin exchanges, payment processors, and users should face.

Finally, policymakers should not only allow Bitcoin's development to continue unimpeded, they should help foster its growth by revisiting existing regulatory barriers. One of the greatest obstacles to Bitcoin's legitimate adoption is the requirement that businesses engaging in money transmission acquire a license from each state. This is a duplicative, laborious, and expensive process that presents a barrier to interstate commerce without much benefit to consumers. Federal lawmakers and regulators should consider whether preemption is necessary.

CONCLUSION

Bitcoin is an exciting innovation that has the potential to greatly improve human welfare and jump-start beneficial and potentially revolutionary developments in payments, communications, and business. Bitcoin's clever use of public-key encryption and peer-to-peer networking solves the double-spending problem that had previously made decentralized digital currencies impossible. These properties combine to create a payment system that could lower transactions costs in business and remittances, alleviate poverty, provide an escape from capital controls and monetary mismanagement, allow for legitimate financial privacy online, and spur new financial innovations. On the other hand, as "digital cash," Bitcoin can be used for money laundering and illicit trade. Banning Bitcoin is not the solution to ending money laundering and illicit trade, just as banning cash is not a solution to these same ills.

Bitcoin could ultimately fail as an experimental digital currency and payment system. An unanticipated problem could arise and undermine the bitcoin economy. A superior cryptocurrency could outcompete and replace Bitcoin. It could simply fizzle out as a fad. The possibilities for failure are endless, but one reason for failure should not be that policymakers did not understand its workings and potential. We are ultimately advocating not for Bitcoin, but for innovation. It is important that policymakers allow this experimentation to continue. Policymakers should work to clarify how Bitcoin is regulated and to normalize its regulation so that we have the opportunity to learn just how innovative Bitcoin can be.

Written Statement to U.S. House of Representatives Committee on Small Business

Thank you Chairman Graves and members of the House Committee on Small Business for the opportunity to appear here today.

My name is Adam White and I'm the Director of Business Development and Sales at Coinbase, a company founded in June 2012 with the goal of making it easy for merchants and consumers to transact with the digital currency, bitcoin. More than 1 million consumers use Coinbase as their bitcoin wallet, and as of today, there are more than 27,000 businesses that entrust Coinbase to accept bitcoin payments on their behalf using our payment tools. These merchants include large, enterprise-level businesses such as Overstock.com and Big Fish Games, as well as a myriad of small businesses like Tealet, Tuft & Needle, and Mondo Cellars.

Prior to my role at Coinbase, I served as a Captain in the United States Air Force and am a veteran of Operation Iraqi Freedom and Operation Enduring Freedom. I also worked briefly as a consultant at Bain & Company and a product manager at Activision Blizzard after completing my MBA at Harvard Business School.

I'd like to begin today by outlining the inherent benefits of Bitcoin in commerce—namely the elimination of fraud, reduction of transaction fees, and monetization of new markets—and how these benefits can be a positive influence on businesses of all sizes.

Bitcoin enables individuals to push payments to merchants without having to share personally identifiable information that can be intercepted by criminals and used for fraudulent purposes. This push functionality gives Bitcoin a unique characteristic that eliminates the risk of fraud, something that merchants, card processors, and banks spend billions of dollars per year combatting. With Bitcoin, for example, the Target data breach that comprised over 70 million consumers' credit card information would not have been possible.

Additionally, many card issuers use fraud detection systems that are overly sensitive to trigger activities for card-not-present transactions. Initial estimates suggest that some merchants turn away nearly eight percent of incoming orders due to suspicious activity, many of which could, in fact, be legitimate. Bitcoin payments are irreversible, so fraudulent charges are prevented from occurring, and as a result, merchants do not bear the risk and cost associated with these false declines.

Due to the elimination of fraud, Bitcoin transactions are dramatically less expensive than traditional card based payments. Merchants can reduce their electronic payments acceptance fees to less than 1% when accepting payment in bitcoin. This is especially important for small businesses that sacrifice anywhere between 3–5% of their revenues in card transaction fees. Businesses can use these savings to reinvest in their company or pass them on to consumers in the form of lower prices. Moreover, merchants are not faced with a fixed fee per transaction, enabling them to forgo minimum transaction limits and sell small ticket items profitability.

Finally, Bitcoin democratizes foreign exchange and enables frictionless, cross-border transactions that settle immediately. Many products and services are not available for sale in foreign countries solely because the business cannot manage the payments systems needed to support overseas commerce. Because of the borderless and global nature of Bitcoin, a bitcoin payment made by customer in New York looks identical to a merchant as a bitcoin payment made by a customer in London, Buenos Aires, or Tokyo. Moreover, there are no international currency conversion fees associated with bitcoin payments so merchants can sell low margin items just as profitably abroad as they do domestically. The ability to easily begin accepting payments from customers around the world can open up whole new markets for merchants, and significantly improve top-line revenue.

We see Bitcoin as an extremely powerful technology, and it is our goal to bring the efficiencies created by the Bitcoin network to the masses. We are encouraged to see the Committee's proactive examination into the topic of bitcoin as it relates to small businesses, and I look forward to engaging in dialogue and answering any questions you may have.

Testimony of Mark T. Williams[1]

Banking Specialist, Commodities and Risk Management Expert

Boston University Finance Department

To U.S. House of Representatives

Committee on Small Business

April 2, 2014

Hearing

Bitcoin: Examining the Benefits and Risks for Small Business

Rayburn House Office Building,

Washington, DC 20515

Introduction

Good afternoon Chairman Sam Graves and other distinguished committee members. My name is Mark Williams and for the last 12 years I have been on the Finance faculty of Boston University where I have specialized in banking, capital markets and risk management related matters. In 2010, I wrote *Uncontrolled Risk,* a book about the fall of Lehman Brothers and what caused the 2008 real estate asset bubble www.uncontrolledrisk.com. Prior to my academic career, I was a senior executive for a Boston-based commodity-trading firm and have worked as a field examiner for the Federal Reserve Bank in San Francisco and Boston. On occasion, I have also been a consultant to small businesses.

Through my academic and work experiences I have gained a strong understanding of how the capital markets function, the role of currency, how businesses operate and how unaddressed risks can result in financial harm. For the last 18 months, I have closely studied, researched, and more recently written on Bitcoin, its structure and its highly-risky nature.

I appreciate the opportunity to testify today and I view this committee room as an extension of the Boston University classroom. My interest and fascination with Bitcoin started in 2011. Initially it was part of an in-class lecture, later a homework assignment, and ultimately, morphed into a full classroom debate. At that time, Bitcoin was trading for 32 cents. Over the last three years, this pseudo currency has taken on a life of its own. In 2013 its speculative value increased from $13 to a market high of $1,200.

Most Recent Events

[1] Mark T. Williams has only a de minimis financial interest in Bitcoin and no direct investment in Bitcoin-related startups.

One month or even one week in the Bitcoin world can be equivalent to a decade in other markets. The price risk associated with Bitcoin is extreme and unlike any other volatile community. Despite the dramatic rise in 2013, prices have not been a one-way space rocket to the moon. Since November 2013, Bitcoin has slid by over 60 percent to $462.[2] China's decision on December 5, 2013 to prohibit its banks and money transmitters from accepting Bitcoin was the pin that has begun to prick the Bitcoin Bubble.[3] On this date, the world's second largest economy warned that virtual currencies carry substantial risk.[4] Other market disruptions have occurred. On January 19, 2014 Alibaba, the Chinese equivalent of Amazon stopped accepting Bitcoin. Two weeks later, Charlie Shrem, the Vice Chairman of the Bitcoin Foundation, located a stone throw from these Chambers, was indicted by the FBI for money laundering. Then on February 6, 2014, Russia declared the use of Bitcoin illegal stating that the Ruble was the sole official currency. That same week, Mt Gox of Japan, formerly the world's largest Bitcoin exchange, accounting for 80 percent of trading volume, announced it had been hacked, and later disclosed customer losses of more than $400 million. The other two major exchanges, Bitstamp, located in Slovenia and BTCe, located in Bulgaria, were also impacted by this attack. The scale and scope of the Mt Gox virtual-bank heist further rattled market confidence, raising new questions about safety and the need for basic consumer protection standards. In February, cyber hackers broke into Silk Road, the defunct deep-web purveyor of illegal goods and services, stealing over $2.7 million worth of e-coins, proving that criminals can also steal from criminals.

On March 11, 2014, the U.S. Financial Industry Regulatory Authority released a stern warning to investors about the dangers of buying and using virtual currencies. Shortly after, on March 24, 2014, the Internal Revenue Service dealt a further blow to Bitcoin, ruling it is not a foreign currency but should be taxed as property. This IRS ruling gives investors with a low-cost basis an added incentive to hoard coins instead of using them for transactional purposes. This further diminishes the already low level of market liquidity. Casting more doubt on the prospects of Bitcoin, on March 14, 2014, famed investor Warren Buffett stated "Stay away. Bitcoin is a mirage." His comments supported remarks made by Charlie Munger, Vice Chairman of Bershire Hathaway a year earlier, when Munger declared Bitcoin "rat poison." [5] Despite these significant market disruptions, scandals and pessimistic comments made by well-respected investors, Bitcoin promoters continue to trumpet the virtues of this volatile, nationless and anonymous currency. Some advocates have declared this period as the Bitcoin Revolution (2000s), equivalent to the early stages of the internet (1990s). Although I do not view Bitcoin as "rat poison," this virtual currency does pose significant risks to small business owners. These risks

[2] Market price of $462 on March 30, 2014 ($738/$1,200) = 62 percent.

[3] On December 4, 2013, former Federal Reserve Bank Chairman Alan Greenspan indicated publically that Bitcoin was a bubble.

[4] China on December 5, 2013 declared that Bitcoin was not a virtual currency but a virtual commodity.

[5] Stated on Fox Business May 6, 2013.

need to be carefully evaluated before deciding whether or not to venture into these new, uncharted waters.

U.S. Small Business - Market Innovation

Small businesses fuel growth. Decisions by owners have broad impact. Presently, U.S. small business accounts for over half of private sector gross domestic product and employment. Since the 1970s, small businesses provide 55 percent of all jobs and 66 percent of all net new jobs. Businesses that are willing to adopt and utilize new technology, such as virtual currencies, may gain a distinct competitive advantage (e.g., cost savings, increased sales) over their competitors. However, blindly adopting technology without understanding the full risk implications can be hazardous to a company's financial health. Bitcoin is an example of new technology that has clear promise, but also poses a multitude of risks for both businesses and consumers.

In my testimony today I will not focus on the promise of virtual currencies as I will leave that to the other hearing witnesses. Instead my focus will be on the significant and currently unaddressed risks associated with Bitcoin. Sound business and regulatory decisions can only be made when these identified risks and promised benefits are examined, and weighed against each other in the light of day.

Once the facts are fully laid out, my hope is to leave this Committee with one simple question to ponder: **what net benefits, if any, does Bitcoin actually provide to legitimate U.S. small businesses?**

How Risky is Bitcoin to Small Businesses?

This question is best summarized by looking at the disclosure statement provided by Coinbase, a San Francisco based money transmitter who is servicing an increasing number of the nation's small businesses. As part of the new account set-up process, Coinbase describes Bitcoin as a virtual currency that could drop to the price of zero. In order to fully assess the risks of Bitcoin, small business owners should take note of this particularly revealing disclosure prior to deciding whether or not to accept Bitcoin. Indeed, if the U.S. dollar carried a similar risk disclaimer, how many small business owners would be willing to use the greenback to conduct commerce?

The 10 Major Risks for U.S. Small Businesses

In determining whether to accept Bitcoin when selling goods and services or for meeting payroll or paying vendors, small business owners need to first assess these 10 major risks. If this panoply of risk is not fully understood or controlled, it has the potential of exposing a business to greater earnings uncertainty, losses and fraud.

These 10 major risks are discussed below.

1. Bitcoin Is Not Legal Tender

Small businesses need to clearly understand that Bitcoin is not legal tender. It is not created or supported by a sovereign—it is nationless. Unlike the U.S. dollar, there are no laws that require businesses or individuals to accept Bitcoin to settle private or public debts. Bitcoin is also not backed by taxing power, ability to assemble an army, assets or other natural resources customarily owned or controlled by nation states. In contrast to legal tender, the use of Bitcoin is limited to those willing to accept it. Presently the group of Bitcoin users is minuscule relative to the U.S. population (1 million out of 317 million). Globally, these numbers are even smaller. If businesses or individuals suddenly decide not to accept it, Bitcoin will become worthless.

Extreme Price Risk

Since inception, Bitcoin has experienced extreme annual price volatility topping 140 percent.[6] Bitcoin is 7 times more risky than gold and 8 times more risky than the S&P 500. Compared to currencies it is 7 times more risky than the unstable Argentinian Peso and 15 times more risky than the U.S. dollar. As a result, it could be argued that small businesses that blindly accept Bitcoin are not actually in commerce but are in the high-risk speculative trading business. In contrast to small businesses, a Wall Street trading company might be willing to assume the triple-digit price risk posed by Bitcoin but only with experienced staff, sophisticated systems, strong controls and a large balance sheet to buffer against daily price swings.

[6] In 2009, annual volatility was approximately 160 percent. Using price data from 2010 forward from Mt Gox, Bitstamp and BTCe, annual volatility through 2014 was approximately 140 percent.

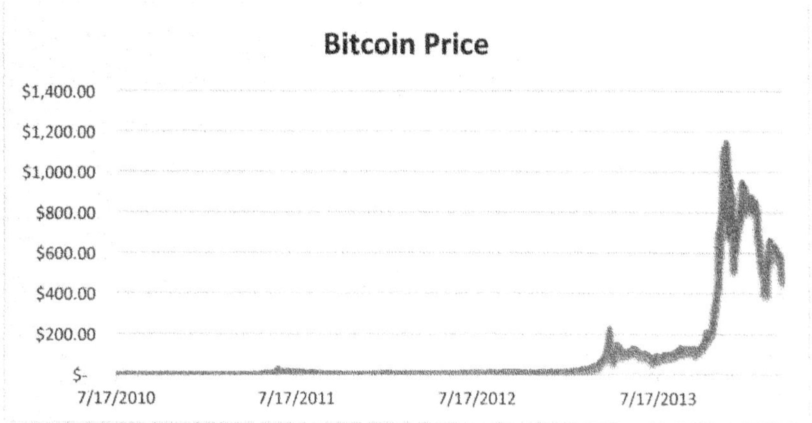

In a single day, it is not uncommon for Bitcoin prices to move by 10 percent. At current price levels, Bitcoin can drop by $50 or more in a single day. In December 2013, in a 48-hour period, Bitcoin plummeted by 50 percent. Since the November 2013 market peak, Bitcoin prices have dropped by over 60 percent. On February

14, 2014, during a flash crash, one block of 6,000 coins fell, in seconds, by over 80 percent to $102 before rebounding.[7]

3. Extreme Price Movements Can Quickly Erase Company Profit Margins

The profit margins of U.S. small businesses are dependent on numerous factors including the nature of the industry, competition, location, number of employees, technology employed, cost of capital and level of management skill and experience. Although net profit margins can be 10 percent or less, more profitable companies earn margins in the 15 to 20 percent range. Examples of higher profit margin professions include CPAs, chiropractors, and dentists, lawyers, portfolio managers and optometrists.[8]

Given that the daily price movement of Bitcoin can be as high as 10 percent, a small business owner who accepts this form of payment could see profit margins reduced or completely erased in a matter of days.

4. Bitcoin is an Asset Bubble in the Process of Deflating

Small business owners need to be cognizant of the fact that Bitcoin prices were only $13 at the start of 2013 and could easily drop to the same low level in the near future. In an efficient capital market, capital flows to its highest and best use as investors seek a tradeoff between desired risk and desired return. When investors receive timely, accurate and transparent information, the likelihood of an asset bubble is diminished. However, even in efficient and well-developed financial market, it is not uncommon to experience bubbles (e.g., Dotcom 2000, Real Estate 2007).

[7] Prices plunged on the BTCe to $102 before rebounding to over $600.
[8] Nelson, Brett, The Most Profitable Small Businesses, Forbes, February 10, 2011.

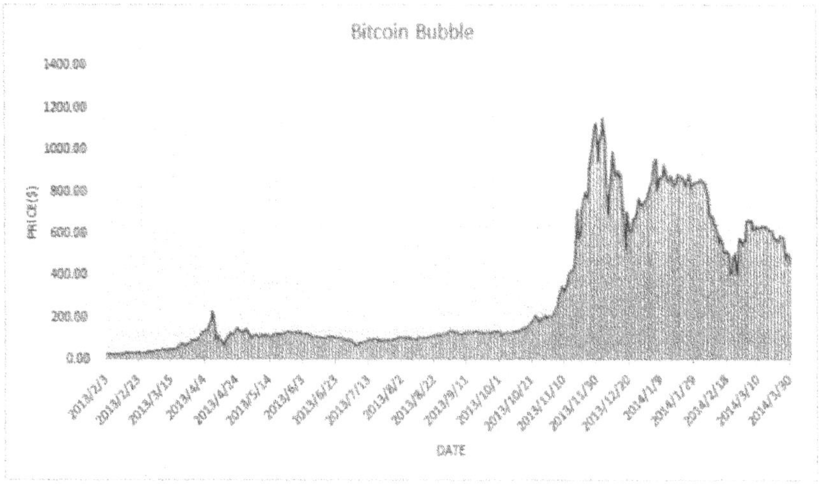

All asset bubbles are similar in that they have three phases: growth, maturity and pop. However, not all asset bubbles see prices collapse during the final phase; sometimes prices deflate over an extended period allowing investors to experience lower losses and softer landings. Bitcoin entered the growth stage in 2011, the maturity stage in 2013 and now is in the pop stage. Since December 2013 rapid price swings continue to demand that owners watch prices on a daily and even hourly basis. If small business owners are willing to accept Bitcoin they need to stay vigilant in monitoring the high probability of a pronounced price collapse.

In December 2013, when prices were still over $1,000, I indicated that Bitcoin could drop to $10 or below (http://cognoscenti.wbur.org/2013/12/05/bitcoin-currency-mark-t-williams). This prediction was based on several observations including the underlying option value of this new and uncertain technology, price level at the start of 2013 and the percentage price drop associated with the 1637 Tulip Mania Bubble [9]. On January 24, 2014, Nobel prize-winner economist Robert Shiller stated "it is a bubble, there is no question about it... it's just an amazing example of a bubble." As articulated by Coinbase, as part of its new customer disclosure statement, business owners have to be prepared for the chance that Bitcoin prices could drop to zero.

5. Growing Concentration and Bankruptcy Risk to Financial Middlemen

Increasingly, small businesses, in an effort to avoid the extreme price risk of Bitcoin, are using the risk-mitigation services of Coinbase and BitPay. However, in relying on these startups, there is a growing exposure to concentration and bankruptcy risk.

Both Coinbase and BitPay, as financial middlemen, accept price risk for a fee and allow businesses to receive their most preferred currency. Merchants are given a fixed Bitcoin conversion rate linked to a window of time. For example, BitPay provides a locked price quote for only 15 minutes. The fee for basic entry level service is 1 percent of transaction value.[10] Customers pay in Bitcoin but merchants can elect to receive U.S. dollars. Extreme daily price swings have created a niche for Coinbase and BitPay but also have created a potentially dangerous level of industry concentration risk. It is important to note that Coinbase and BitPay do not eliminate overall Bitcoin price risk but simply warehouse this risk on their books. This is of particular concern given that these two fledgling firms are lightly regulated, thinly capitalized, and not required to operate with minimum capital requirements. Without these important safeguards, it is uncertain what this price mitigation guarantee is really worth? Adding to this concentration risk, no derivatives market exists to off-load this significant risk.

As the number of small business customers increases, the amount of Bitcoin price-risk retained by these financial middlemen will also grow. For Coinbase or BitPay, a single-day price drop of 20 percent or a prolonged price decline on a large enough Bitcoin position could be financially devastating.[11]

Coinbase also has multiple business lines that present an inherent conflict of interest. In offering price-risk mitigation and Bitcoin-for-sale services, Coinbase has an economic incentive to sell Bitcoin at the highest market price while customers have an economic in-

[9] The price dropped once the bubble burst was 99 percent.

[10] BitPay has a four tier customer structure with fees ranging as low as 1 percent of transaction value to monthly fees of up to $3,000 for extremely large transactions.

[11] Since December 2013, there have been several days where daily intra and inter-day price movements have exceeded 10 percent, increasing to 15, 20 percent or more.

centive to buy Bitcoin at the lowest market price. Without strong regulatory oversight it is unclear how Coinbase effectively balances this duel and conflicted loyalty.

If these financial middlemen were to declare bankruptcy, no longer able to honor their obligations, and accounts receivable owed to merchants were not paid, such a scenario could be extremely costly.

6. <u>Bitcoin Exchange Bankruptcy Risk</u>

Business owners can also sell coins and open e-wallets through Bitcoin exchanges. Since Mt Gox trading was halted on February 7, 2014, and its subsequent bankruptcy two weeks later, the bulk of Bitcoin trading has been concentrated in the hands of two exchanges: Bitstamp and BTCe. To sell on these exchanges, U.S. small businesses must send instructions and trust that their requests will be honored. These exchanges operate under no regulation and are outside of the reach of U.S. regulators. With no regulatory oversight, it is not unusual for certain well connected buyers and sellers to gain preferential treatment in terms of price execution. Front-running is not uncommon.[12] In a weak corporate governance environment are customer funds adequately protected from internal or external fraud? In this "wild-west" atmosphere many exchanges have failed. It is estimated that of the 40 Bitcoin exchanges that have been started since the inception of Bitcoin, almost half (18) have failed.[13] When exchanges close, customers tend to lose everything. In November 2013, GBL, based in Hong Kong, closed its doors, costing investors over $4 million. In December 2013, the European Banking Authority also warned of the dangers of other exchanges failing and of the lack of investor protection laws. Should one or both of these exchanges go into bankruptcy, small businesses that store e-coins on either of these exchanges could experience substantial financial exposure.

7. <u>Bitcoin Use Can Trigger Significant Tax Risk</u>

Unlike legal tender, Bitcoin has been designated for tax purposes as property. This distinction is significant. Unlike legal tender, when accepting Bitcoin, business owners can be subject to additional taxes associated with the gains—the difference in value on date received versus value on date sold.

On March 25, 2014, IRS issued a ruling that clarified the tax treatment of Bitcoin but, in doing so, created greater uncertainty about the e-coin's future. Bitcoin is now taxed as property and not as foreign currency. Any gains in Bitcoin value is taxed as ordinary income (as high as 39.6 percent) or at the capital gains (20 percent) tax rate. Given the high price run-up of Bitcoin during 2013, there are significant tax considerations which also influence the level of hoarding versus spending. If an e-coin was purchased for $250 and it now trades for $500, the owner is going to be less motivated to use it for transactional currency purposes, especially if doing so

[12] Practice of a self-interested firm executing trades in its own account after having advanced market information, sometimes trading at the detriment of the customer positions.

[13] Moore, Tyler, Christin, Nicolas, Beware the Middleman: Empirical Analysis of Bitcoin-Exchange Risk, 2013.

would trigger an additional tax event. For holders of Bitcoin, this IRS ruling reduces the incentive to use e-coins for transactional purposes, reducing transaction flow, market liquidity and price stability. Prior to this ruling, over 90 percent of e-coins were hoarded. It is highly plausible this tax ruling will encourage even more hoarding.

Small business owners are now confronted with several other tax risks. If they decide to accept and retain Bitcoin, they will need to keep records of the market price on the day received and sold. Any increase in value from that date forward would be subject to income tax. If a merchant decided to pay its employees in Bitcoin, the firm also needs to withhold the required employment tax in U.S. dollars. Companies that pay employees in Bitcoin are also subjecting staff to increased tax risk should coins appreciate in value or if prices drop. Such a policy, given Bitcoin's extreme daily price volatility, would unfairly penalize employees.

8. Transaction Fraud Risk - Double Spending

Under Bitcoin protocol all new transactions are validated through the blockchain, a public ledger that is independently verified every 10 minutes. Validation is done to avoid a situation where a customer is able to fraudulently double-spend this e-coin. However, this 10 minute window poses potential risk should two businesses be paid with the same Bitcoin. If a double-spending incident occurred during this time gap, the last merchant to report the transaction would have little recourse to collect on this payment.[14] That merchant would then lose the value of the product or services sold. If the customer had used a credit card and not Bitcoin to commit the fraud, the business would have had recourse through the credit card company. One way merchants can attempt to mitigate this risk is by waiting until a full validation is completed before permitting customers to receive goods or services.

9. Bitcoin Slow Transaction Speed Increases Credit Risk

Credit cards such as Visa and MasterCard have higher upfront charges for small businesses; however, the transaction speed of the credit card network is superior to the existing transaction speed of Bitcoin. At point-of-sale, it still remains faster and more convenient for customers to swipe a card or input the card number on an internet e-commerce site than it is to use Bitcoin. The process of copying and pasting an e-coin alphanumeric string into another program and waiting for the confirmation is cumbersome and time-consuming. Merchants are also much more accustomed to receiving a point-of-sale credit card authorization and receipt within seconds of sale. With Bitcoin, merchants remain exposed if they deliver product or services before payment confirmation is fully verified.

On the existing Bitcoin network, only 7 transactions per second can be processed compared to 2,000 transactions on the credit card

[14] Although the Bitcoin community has indicated that double-spending events are rare, and controls against it are strong, merchants still need to be prepared should such fraud be committed.

network.[15] If the number of Bitcoin transactions on the existing network continues to grow, and if the network is not accordingly scaled up, small businesses accepting Bitcoin could see transaction time lengthened and payment verification slowed. Although inconvenient for customers, to mitigate this risk, merchants may need to have customers wait until a transaction can be completely verified.

BitPay, a virtual currency payment facilitator provides small businesses with three speed setting to help manage the Bitcoin payment confirmation process. At the fastest speed, merchants assume total credit risk if they deliver the product in advance of receiving a completely verified payment confirmation. For small transactions like candy, coffee and newspapers this concern may be minimal. For larger transactions, the concern for credit risk may take precedence over customer inconvenience. This is especially true before retail customers are allowed to take possession of merchandise or a product is shipped from an internet-based enterprise.

10. Risk of E-Wallet Theft Remains High

Small business owners that decide to accept Bitcoin have to create an e-wallet, and determine whether to store it on one's own personal computer hard drive or relying on a third-party vendor such as Blockchain or Coinbase. Third-party vendors that create and hold e-wallets perform a deposit-type function. However, unlike banks, these vendors lack regulatory oversight, minimum capital standards and don't provide consumer protection against loss or theft. Once created, e-wallets generate a public and private key. Small businesses need to have strong controls in place around the storage of e-wallets and of the private key.[16] This is particularly important given that Bitcoin is an anonymous currency that is irreversible once transferred.[17] Bitcoin features make it an ideal target for cyber criminals. If an e-wallet is hacked and coins stolen or transferred by mistake, they are lost forever. If a computer is infected with a virus, it could wipe out the hard drive and the stored value of all e-coins.

Relying on third-party vendors also has it drawbacks, as it requires confidence that adequate controls are in place to minimize the likelihood of cyber-attacks or internal employee fraud. It is not uncommon for e-wallet service providers to go out of business. This was evidenced by the dramatic and costly Mt Gox bankruptcy in February 2014. Last month, Flexcoin, a Bitcoin e-wallet bank, based in Canada also folded after being hit by a devastating cyber-attack.

Background

a) Forms of Payment

[15] Bitcoin advocates claim that in the future the Bitcoin payment network will be much quicker than the existing credit card network. However in 2014, transaction processing time for Bitcoin remains much slower as measured in time to confirmation.

[16] Some businesses to gain maximum control have taken paper copies of private keys and placed then in locked boxes, E-wallets can also be taken off line. This control technique is called storage.

[17] These secrecy features also raise the question of what business need these benefits unless they have something they want to hide.

Forms of payment in commerce have evolved over many centuries including barter, shells, crude metal coins, precious metal coins, leather money, paper money, wampum, gold, gold-backed dollars, charge plates, checks, wires, credit cards, debit cards and prepaid cards. Each manifestation has occurred in response to consumer demand for more convenient ways to conduct commerce. In the process, businesses have expanded and financially benefited.

Virtual currencies, Bitcoin in particular, are being presented as the newest attempt at payment innovation. Bitcoin promoters claim it is a safer, faster and cheaper form of payment than existing forms including credit cards. These claims have yet to be fully proven.

b) <u>Facilitating Commerce</u>

It is widely known that businesses can increase sales by expanding the availability of customer payment options. Credit cards remain the primary form of payment used by consumers when entering brick and mortar businesses or when shopping online. Unlike cash or debit cards, credit cards facilitate greater purchasing by delivering a fast, short-term loan to consumers. In a cash only economy, businesses would not sell as many products or services, and profits would fall. Credit cards also increase impulse buying. To encourage even greater purchasing, some credit card companies establish reward programs, enhance product warranties and provide free loss/damage insurance on products purchased. In addition to credit cards, PayPal makes it convenient for customers by providing the option of quickly transferring money from either personal bank accounts or credit cards.[18] PayPal has made significant inroads into e-commerce, now representing 18 percent of the market or $315.3 million in daily payment activity.

The cost of processing plastic is higher and small businesses attempt to manage higher fees especially on smaller purchased items by imposing credit card minimums or by establishing a cash or credit card price. The average cost of credit card transactions to merchants ranges from 2 to 3 percent. In the last year, small businesses have also gained greater relief from credit card fees. Since January 27, 2013, U.S. merchants have been permitted to pass on to consumers a surcharge when using a credit card. Presently, few merchants have exercised this right.

Small businesses have also received meaningful fee relief when accepting debit cards. Since the Dodd Frank Act and with the adoption of the Durbin Amendment, per-swipe fees have dropped by about 50 percent to 21 cents. This cost savings of an estimated $8 billion per year has been advantageous to small business.

c) <u>Credit Cards Fees Come With Merchant Benefits</u>

Credit cards have fees but with these fees come services and benefits to both merchants and customers. Consumers using credit cards are more likely to spend than those who only have cash. Business owners at point-of-sale receive instantaneous assurance

[18] The predecessor company to PayPal was founded in December 1999. On October 3, 2002, PayPal became a wholly owned subsidiary of eBay.

that a card is valid and its owner has sufficient funds available to make a purchase. Credit card companies also work with merchants to reduce the change of fraudulent purchases. Consumer sales are increased through the use of loyalty program, enhanced guarantees and damage insurance. As a financial middleman, credit card companies also handle dispute resolution, gathering facts from merchants and customers. The chargeback protection (disputed purchases) also increases the likelihood of credit card use and thus a greater number of purchases.

d) Evolving Payment Landscape - Business Transactions

Currently, two-thirds of all point-of-sales transactions in the U.S. are completed either with credit, debit or gift cards. A little over twenty-five percent of sales are completed with cash and this rate is projected to decline to only 23 percent by 2017.[19] Technology continues to make it easier for merchants to accept credit card transactions as older swipe machines and dedicated phone lines continue to disappear. Innovative firms such as Square, WePay and PayPal are making it more convenient to accept plastic or to make bank account direct transfers.

There is also significant growth in the use of prepaid cards. In 2013, Starbucks reported that one-third of the company's U.S. sales or $2.5 billion was conducted through this payment method. Annually, over $65 billion in U.S. sales is conducted through prepaid cards. This convenient and inexpensive payment method is projected to double in consumer use in the next two years.

Most Small Businesses Don't Accept Credit Cards

Internet commerce continues to grow rapidly where the preferred payment methods are either credit card or the use of PayPal-type services. In 2013, U.S. E-commerce sales increased by 17.22 percent to $380.6 billion accounting for 6 percent of total sales. Despite this market trend, more than half (55%) of the nation's 27 million small businesses do not accept credit cards.[20] Some businesses argue that credit card-related fees (2 to 3%) or PayPal fees (2.2. to 2.9%) remain too high, while other small companies prefer cash over the transparency and reporting requirements associated with the use of credit cards.

Cash-only businesses also increase the chance for tax under-reporting. The Internal Revenue Service estimated that under-reporting by small businesses represents about $140 billion in annual uncollected taxes. It is also estimated that 56 percent of sole proprietors' cash receipts are not disclosed for tax purposes. Since 2012, the IRS has devoted more resources to address tax under-reporting by small businesses.[21]

Why Small Businesses Might Utilize Bitcoin?

[19] Javelin Strategy & Research 2012.

[20] McClue, TJ., Why Don't More Small Businesses Accept Credit Cards, Forbes, August 16, 2013.

[21] IRS requires payment processors to annually file form 1099-k, a record of system transaction history.

There are two major reasons why U.S. small businesses might either accept Bitcoin as payment and/or use it for paying employees, and vendors:

1. Illegitimate Purposes - Silk Road, the deep web purveyor of drugs, guns and prostitution, accepted payment only in Bitcoin. The FBI shutdown Silk Road in October of 2013. The Silk Road Case elevated public awareness of Bitcoin as the designer currency of choice for the criminally-inclined. The anonymous nature of Bitcoin and the fact that transactions are irreversible, make it an ideal way for criminals to launder money, buy illicit goods and avoid taxation with little chance of detection.

Legitimate Purposes

a. Gain Marketing Exposure - Bitcoin has gained increased media attention. As a result, more small businesses view accepting Bitcoin as a way to gain market exposure. Posting a sign on a door front, on a website or gaining local media coverage increases free advertising and brand awareness. For example, Grass Hill Alpacas, a Massachusetts lama farm and purveyor of wool socks, has gained considerable visibility being an early acceptor of Bitcoin.

b. Reduce Transaction Costs and Gain New Customers - Bitcoin represents a new possibly less expensive, private payment form to sell goods and services and possibly expanding sales by reaching new customers.

How do Small Businesses Obtain Bitcoin?

There are four legitimate ways businesses can obtain Bitcoin:

1. Buying through an exchange (BTCe) or money transmitter (e.g., Coinbase)
2. Accepting as a form of payment for goods and services
3. Receiving as a gift
4. Mining coins

To obtain Bitcoin, assuming there is no interest in mining coins, businesses first have to setup e-wallets, either through third-party vendors (e.g., Blockchain) or by storing them on the hard drive of a personal computer, which then allows for the receiving and sending of coins.

Additional Background

There are over 190 virtual currencies traded in the marketplace totaling $6.5 billion in stated value. http://coinmarketcap.com/mineable.html. Of these traded e-currencies, Bitcoin, is the dominant player representing about $6 billion or 92 percent of this total stated value.

In 2009, a programmer by the pseudonym Satoushi Nakamoto[22] supposedly designed Bitcoin, a computer generated "virtual cur-

[22] In March, Newsweek presented facts in an attempt to prove the founder in Dorian S. Nakamoto who currently lives east of Los Angeles. When confronted by reporters, Mr. Nakamoto denied having any connection with the creation of Bitcoin.

rency" produced by solving progressively complex mathematical equations.[23] The code-protocol for Bitcoin is open source, allowing it to be easily viewed, commented on and if a majority of programmers agree, changes are adopted. In this regard, Bitcoin is very transparent.[24] Bitcoin, the pseudo currency and Bitcoin, the low-cost payment system, are dependent on each other and are inseparable. Bitcoin is the locomotive while the payment system is the track that allows it to move back and forth. The Bitcoin infrastructure is decentralized and based on a peer-to-peer structure. Individuals in a multitude of locations, using powerful computers to solve pre-determined equations, authenticate e-coins and help keep a general ledger of ongoing transactions. A continuous blockchain is used and maintained to record Bitcoin ownership. New transactions are authenticated every ten minutes. Unlike in credit card transactions, the peer-to-peer network was designed to eliminate the need for the financial middleman or the associated fees. These individuals verify transactions and provide the backbone control to ensure that e-coins are authentic and are not double-spent. As a reward for their efforts, they earn blocks of e-coins. This process is referred to as mining and those that do it are called miners. Interestingly, using such terminology also gives the false impression that something of tangible value is being created such as gold being mined out of the ground. Some enthusiasts have claimed that Bitcoin is gold for geeks. Initially, the entry-level barrier to become a miner was low. Overtime, this barrier has risen and those who are already mining have a competitive advantage and greater market power.

At first miners were rewarded with 50 coins per block. Initially Bitcoin prices were in pennies. More recently, a block is equal to 25 coins. The block/coin ratio will continue to halve as time goes on. It takes approximately 10 minutes to mine a block and approximately 4,000 new e-coins are generated globally per day. Currently over 12.3 million Bitcoins have been minted and by year 2140, the 21 million limit will be reached. A preset quantity limitation creates scarcity which puts upward pressure on price. This is especially true as long as new investors can be recruited to buy newly minted e-coins. Although commodity scarcity is dictated by predetermined rules, it is unclear what mechanism or controls are in place to guarantee that rules will be followed and that incentives to cheat the system will be eliminated.

Theoretically, the Bitcoin mining and authenticity process is decentralized, keeping collusion between miners to a minimum.[25] As new e-coins are minted they are added to the blockchain and when trades occur, existing e-coins are authenticated against this blockchain. As more Bitcoins are mined, the blockchain grows longer in complexity and the verification time increases. In Feb-

---

[23] Bitcoin has not been recognized by any of the G20 countries as meeting the definition of currency as it lacks price stability and does not provide a stable store of value. As a result it is a speculative virtual commodity with no tangible value.

[24] The Bitcoin community has argued that this open source unregulated peer-to-peer approach is a strong control as it allows a large community of computer scientists, software engineers and cryptologists to watch over the system and insure its integrity.

[25] However, in practice, as prices have skyrocketed, there has been a greater economic incentive for miners to band together in pursuit of increased profits. As a result, this remains a clear weakness in the Bitcoin infrastructure.

ruary 2014, a series of cyber-attacks occurred on the Bitcoin infrastructure, targeting three of the largest exchanges, resulting in significant trading disruption. While the integrity of the blockchain remained intact, several third-party vendors were significantly impacted. Mt Gox eventually filed bankruptcy and the other two largest exchanges, Bitstamp and BTCe were immobilized for a week. During this attack, markets and Bitcoin prices suffered.

Bitcoin: Examining the Benefits and Risks for Small Business

U. S. House Committee On Small Business

April 2, 2014

L. Michael Couvillion, Ph.D.
Plymouth State University
Plymouth, NH 033264

Principal Effects on Small Business

- Bitcoin is a practical and successful reality in the current world in which small businesses operate.
- Bitcoin is potentially very disruptive to existing business models, whether the model describes consumer, business, employees, governments, or regulators.
- Small businesses that are considering Bitcoin must consider the steep learning and implementation curves inherent in this new and unfamiliar technology.
- Bitcoin 's fundamental promise lies in its ability to reduce transactions costs for organizations that adopt it, including new e-commerce businesses and non-profit organizations.
- Compared with existing payments processes, Bitcoin can enhance security, but only if best practices for its implementation are followed.

Financial Advantages

- Bitcoin makes possible very secure cash flow payments, especially if existing 2 Factor Authentification practices are used.
- Compared with credit/debit cards, small businesses that implement Bitcoin may incur lower startup costs.
- Small entities that choose to hold Bitcoin balances may realize speculative gains (or losses) as the dollar price per Bitcoin fluctuates. For the time period May 14, 2013 to March 18, 2014 the annualized return is 207%
- Because chargebacks are virtually eliminated, the merchant can expect the prompt receipt of almost all sales revenue.
- Bitcoin represents a much cheaper payment processing system compared with credit/debit cards. Its swipe fee is $0.15 compared with $0.25 for credit cards, and a typical Bitcoin wallet provider has a 1% fee compared with about 3% for credit cards. This results in cash flows which are between 7.5% (for micro sales) and 1.6% (for large sales) higher If a customer chooses to pay with Bitcoin rather than a credit card. The table below compares the expense:

Some Cost Comparisons - BTC vs. Credit Cards

CC Sale in $$$	Micro - $1	Small - $10	Typical - $100	Large - $10,000
Swipe Fee	$0.25	$0.25	$0.25	$0.25
3% Visa/MC/Disc.	$0.03	$0.30	$3.00	$300.00
Bid Ask %	$0.00	$0.00	$0.00	$0.00
Total Fees	$0.28	$0.55	$3.25	$3.00
% of Sale	28.0%	5.50%	3.25%	3.00%
Net Sale	$0.72	$9.45	$96.75	$9,699.75

BTC Sale in $$$	Micro - $1	Small - $10	Typical - $100	Large - $10,000
Swipe Fee	$0.15	$0.15	$0.15	$0.15
1% Bitcoin Wallet	$0.01	$0.10	$1.00	$100.00
Bid Ask % -.40%	$0.01	$0.01	$0.40	$40.00
Total Fees	$0.17	$0.26	$1.55	$140.15
% of Sale	17.0%	2.60%	1.55%	1.40%
Net Sale	$0.83	$9.74	$98.45	$9,859.85

- Bitcoin daily returns do not correlate with those of other financial assets. Four distinct assets were analyzed for any potential relationship to Bitcoin: US Stock Market (SPY), Short-Term Global Interest Rates (MINT), Emerging Markets Currency (CEW), and the US Dollar Index (UUP). In each case, the single-factor models show that no connection was demonstrated with very high levels of confidence. This lack of a strong relationship makes Bitcoin a potentially valuable hedge for businesses with exposure to these risk factors.

Financial Disadvantages

- Bitcoin is a 100% digital method of remittances. Therefore, any small business that chooses to use it must have reliable access to the Internet whenever any transaction is initiated.
- The business must link its business checking account with a traditional bank to the accounts of the online wallet provider. This link enables seamless transfer of cash to Bitcoin and vice versa. If its commercial bank is reluctant to do business with a Bitcoin entity some integration problems will occur. Such problems are more likely with overseas banks than US banks.
- In the past, many Bitcoin exchanges have failed. If a small business chooses to use an exchange that is not professionally managed and does not employ best security practice, it is possible that Bitcoin exchange balances might be compromised as the affairs of the failed exchange are resolved. Since the exchange may well be located in a non-US country, such resolution can take many months and result in significant loss of working capital for the small businesses and customers affected.

- Standard financial tools are of limited value to regulators and other market participants. The root problem is that the underlying data do **not** conform to the assumptions which are commonly made to assess risk and return. In particular, the assumption of a normal distribution for Bitcoin daily price returns is not valid. Its distribution is rather skewed right, has a pronounced peak, and contains numerous outliars ("fat tails") or extreme observations.

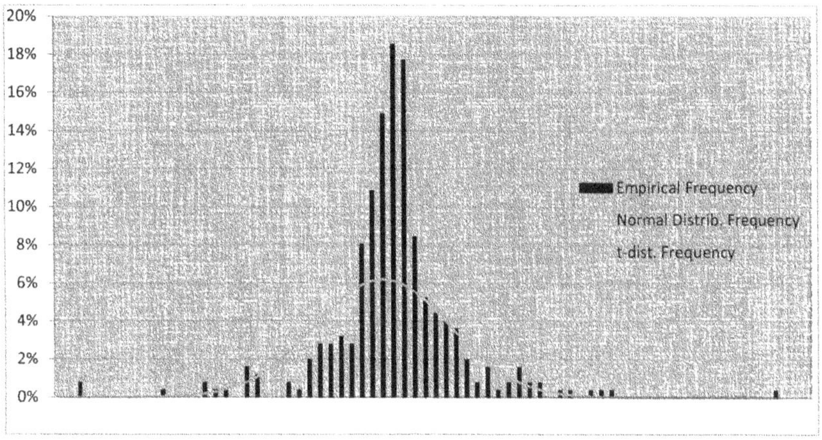

Goodness-of-fit tests indicate that the above distribution is neither normal, t-distributed, lognormal, or uniform. Because of this limitation, it will be difficult for financial regulators to use traditional tools such as Value at Risk to effectively conduct stress tests. This limitation also makes it more difficult for asset managers to limit risk budgets and to optimize portfolios. Covariance matrices become unstable. Bitcoin price predictions are much more difficult to make accurately.

- Bitcoin exhibits extreme price volatility. In fact, compared with the US stock market (S&P500) the standard deviation of Bitcoin returns is 129% vs. 11% and is thus 12x higher. While its reward-to-risk ratio (Sharpe Ratio) is 1.61 and comparable to that of the S&P500 (1.50) should a small business be unable or unwilling to convert BTC to currency at the point and time of sale it is likely that the dollar value of the sale could be very different than expected. The chart below shows the price history of Bitcoin from May 2013 to March 2014:

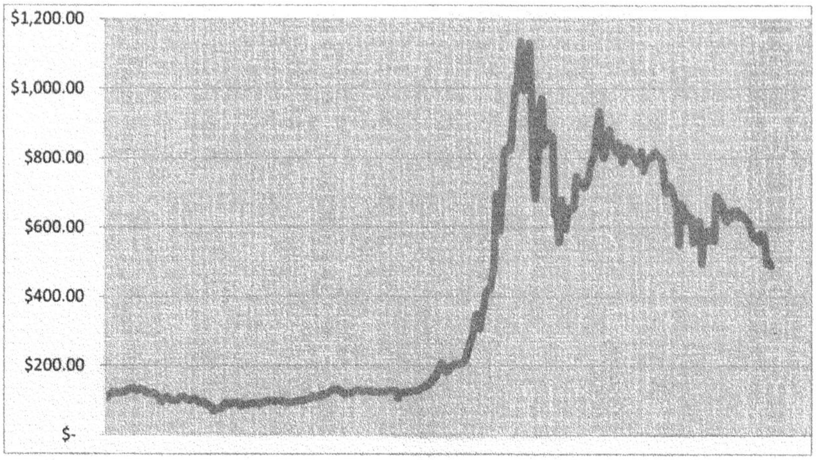

Another way to study the price volatility of Bitcoin is to examine day-to-day movements in its dollar price. For this time period, the largest positive price move was about 37% and the largest negative was 31%. Such price swings are far larger than chance would suggest. The chart below depicts the history of these daily returns. The autocorrelation coefficient is significant at the 5% level and is -0.146, suggesting that large upward daily price swings are slightly more likely to be followed by negative swings than chance would predict.

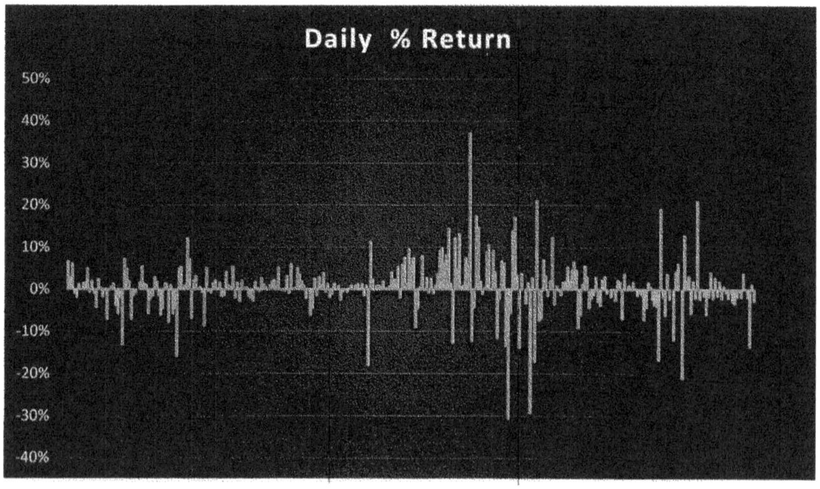

Nonfinancial Advantages

- Large-scale data breaches that have affected millions of credit card users are almost impossible with Bitcoin use . Retail use cases are an important application in which Bitcoin is safer to use than credit/debit cards.
- Confirmation of transactions can occur very quickly for merchants who use Bitcoin, often in just a few minutes.
- Chargebacks do not occur for Bitcoin merchants unless the merchant decides to grant a refund. While this makes the cash flow more certain, the consumer at present has no recourse should a charge be contested.
- At least for now, Bitcoin is considered trendy by younger consumers. This factor helps to differentiate a new small business from its competition.
- Bitcoin is specifically designed for E-commerce applications. It thus represents an easy and inexpensive way for a small business to attract interest in its website.
- The blockchain makes messaging possible.. In this way it represents another way for small businesses to communicate with their customers.

Nonfinancial Disadvantages

- The technology is simple to implement and inexpensive for small businesses. However, employees must be trained in its use and in how to answer questions from customers.
- Likewise, at least at first some businesses must educate their customers.
- Resistance from existing banks and suppliers who do not wish to do business with a Bitcoin accepting firm could be a problem which is not necessarily easy to solve.
- Every transaction, no matter how small, is encoded permanently in the blockchain. While this feature makes it possible to conduct triple-entry accounting processes and helps to perform audits, it does represent a problem for small businesses who do not wish to have their transactions noted.
- The regulatory status of Bitcoin, especially in the US, is uncertain. Different regulators have taken different positions on the use of Bitcoin, such as:
  A. State governments have adopted a wide variety of different regulations regarding Bitcoin use in their state.
  B. The Federal Reserve System has no current plans to regulate Bitcoin as long as current statutes regarding Know Your Customer and Anti-Money Laundering are followed.
  C. The Internal Revenue Service has just issued taxpayer guidance which provides for differing tax treatment of Bitcoin transactions depending on the use case and intent of the taxpayer.

Predictions

- Digital currency is here to stay and will ultimately thrive as partial substitutes for credit cards and fiat currency.
- Consumer and small business ease-of-use will steadily improve as smart phone apps seamlessly integrate to facilitate the exchange of BTC between consumer and business coin wallets.
- Businesses that are early adopters will have a real first- mover advantage over more cautious competitors.
- Governments will monitor developments and find ways to apply existing regulatory principles to this market. A partnership between the Bitcoin Foundation and the public sector will collaboratively establish best practices for implementation.
- Federal taxation is now established as the IRS implements its new guidelines. State taxation is not likely but is possible in some jurisdictions.
- The market price of Bitcoin follows a Random Walk. The price series is integrated of order 1. The best single predictor of the price of a Bitcoin tomorrow is 99.2% of its price today plus $4.73. With a model standard error of $40.115, we can be fairly certain (95%) that the price in the future will be within these bounds, assuming a starting value of $500. The price range tomorrow will then be $421 -- $579. In 46 days, the price range expands to $1,000 -- $0. If the current price volatility moderates over time, Bitcoin has a bright future.

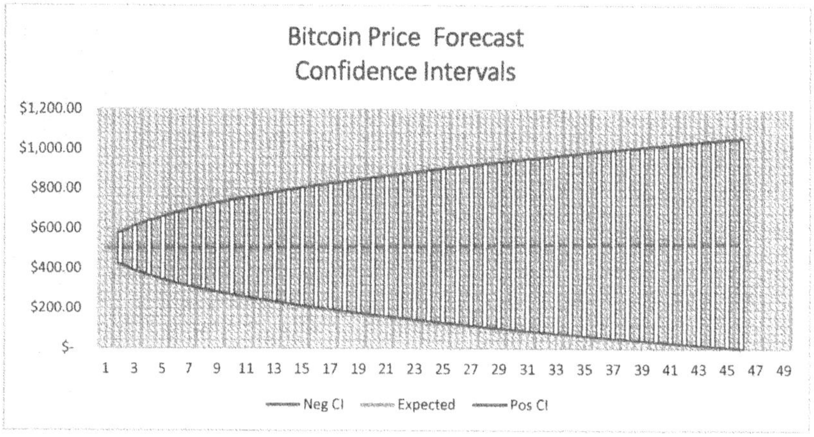

www.ingramcontent.com/pod-product-compliance
Lightning Source LLC
Chambersburg PA
CBHW080720190526
45169CB00006B/2445
* 9 7 8 1 5 3 3 6 9 1 4 9 1 *